Cradled in Human Hands

A Textbook on Environmental Responsibility

Eileen P. Flynn

Sheed & Ward

In loving memory of
my mother and father
Ellen and John Francis Flynn

Sheed & Ward™ is a service of National Catholic Reporter Publishing Company, Inc.

Library of Congress Catalog Card Number: 90-63483

ISBN: 1-55612-413-9

Published by: Sheed & Ward
115 E. Armour Blvd. P.O. Box 419492
Kansas City, MO 64141-6492

To order, call: (800) 333-7373

Contents

1. An Endangered Planet
Dangers which Threaten the Earth 3
The Atmosphere is Endangered 15
The Waters are Endangered 25
Conclusion 30
Exercise 31
Questions for Discussion 33
For Further Reading 34
Glossary 34

2. Making an Ethical Case for Environmental Responsibility
Traditional Approach to Environmental Responsibility:
   Anthropocentrism 43
Alternate Approaches to Environmental Responsibility:
   A Non-anthropocentric or Egalitarian Ethic 48
   Deep Ecology and Ecofeminism 52
Ten Commandments of Non-anthropocentric
   Environmentalism 56
Formulating a Coherent Ethical Response 57
Reasons for Responsible Behavior toward the
   Environment 59
Conclusion 63
Questions for Discussion 66
Debate 67
For Further Reading 67
Glossary 67

3. The Role of Religious Insight in the Formation of a Response to the Environmental Crisis
Connection between the Judeo-Christian Tradition and the
   Environmental Crisis 74
Religious Insight of Eastern and Native American
   Religions 88
New Perspectives in Christian Theology 91
A Stumbling Block 99
Conclusion 99
Exercise 100
Questions for Discussion 102
Debate 103

For Further Reading 103
Glossary 104

4. Business, Government and the Environment
Developing a Corporate Conscience 110
Industrial Pollution and Waste 113
Industrial Response to Dwindling Resources 118
Agriculture and the Challenge of Sustainability 122
Motivating Business and Agriculture to be
    Environmentally Responsible 126
Governmental Interaction with Industry
    and Agriculture 128
Conclusion 133
Case Study 134
Questions for Discussion 136
Debate 137
For Further Reading 137
Glossary 138

5. The Individual and Commitment to the Common Good
Overcoming Negativism 141
Becoming Committed to the Common Good 143
Exercising Care and Concern for the Environment . . . 146
Becoming Committed to Advocacy 149
Conclusion 151
Case Study 152
Questions for Discussion 153
Debate 154
For Further Reading 154

Chapter One

An Endangered Planet

Introduction

Humans coinhabit planet earth with a mind-boggling array of other species. The way in which humans live and act profoundly affects the rest of the *ecosphere* because of the sometimes subtle and sometimes obvious interdependencies between and among species as well as the ways humans are able to alter these interdependencies. For example, if *deforestation* takes place, it is obvious that some birds will lose their nesting places and some people their firewood. The air pollution which results from deforestation may seem less obvious, but it too would be a direct result of the removal of the trees. This is because trees which once took in carbon dioxide to use in the process of photosynthesis no longer do so, resulting in more carbon dioxide remaining in the atmosphere, which may cause, as we shall see, many deleterious effects.

Based on radioactive dating of lunar rocks and meteorites, scientists theorize that the earth is 4.5 to 5 billion years old, and they estimate that the human species has inhabited the earth for approximately 300,000 years.[1] Although all phases of human history have been marked by deliberate interventions in ecological processes, it is the period since the *Industrial Revolution* in which the most significant and far-reaching interventions have taken place, giving cause for today's growing concern about the well-being of the environment. In the United States we are beginning to realize that all the many industries which form the backbone of our capitalist economy, as well as some of the technologies which have been introduced to enhance agricultural production, have resulted in erosion and/or pollution of the soil and its fruit, as well as pollution of the air and the waters. We are also learning how costly and difficult it is to clean up pollution caused by improper disposal of toxic wastes. And we are coming to understand that our affluent First World lifestyle is environmentally problematic: we drive cars, we eat meat,* and we live hundreds (sometimes thousands) of miles from the land on which our food is grown. We keep warm by burning *fossil fuels* for heat in the winter and turn to our air conditioners for relief in the hot weather. We generate 438,000 tons of garbage per day.

Growth in the earth's human population is also a reason for concern. Population has increased from an estimated 1.3 billion in 1850 to an estimated 2.49 billion in 1950 and an estimated 4.3 billion in 1980.[2] According to the United Nations Fund for Population Activities, the world's population is now estimated at 5.3 billion and it will likely reach 6.25 billion by the year 2000.[3]

When we walk in a park on a clear sunny day and feel the refreshment of a delightful breeze, we tend to deny that there are any big, difficult, deeply-rooted environmental problems. On the other hand, when we feel sickened by the air pollution in a city on the occasion of a particularly serious smog alert, we tend to think that our environmental problems are so complex and entrenched as to defy human attempts at a solution. My thesis is that humankind must embark upon the mammoth undertaking of stabilizing and restoring the environment of our endangered planet, and that stabilization and restoration constitute a difficult but achievable goal. The first step to be taken on this journey is to become informed about the dangers which threaten the earth, and it is to this task that we now turn.

---

* It takes 16 pounds of grain and soybeans and 2,500 gallons of water to produce one pound of beef. And cattle ranching accounts for a good chunk of the rain forest destruction in Central America.

Dangers Which Threaten the Earth

The Soil Is Endangered

We have a tendency to underestimate the value of the soil, and to take the soil for granted. Sometimes lists of environmental concerns do not even include soil; such omissions, however, are serious oversights. Humans depend directly and indirectly on fertile soil for most of the food and some of the drink which compose their diet. Animals are also dependent on the soil, as are the plants, trees and shrubs which are rooted therein. The environmental challenge which the soil presents to humans is that, if fertile, its fertility be maintained so that it can bring forth repeated harvests at similar yields far into the future. And, if the fertility of the soil has been depleted, measures need to be taken to restore its fertility. The overarching goal is to attain sustainability, that is, that the agricultural system be able to maintain sufficient productivity to meet the worldwide need for produce even in the face of major disturbances such as soil erosion, unanticipated droughts or the appearance of new pests.

Soil is the collection of chemical and biotic materials, mixed with varying amounts of air and water, which forms the relatively thin layer that comprises the medium in which vegetation grows. An inch of fertile topsoil takes from 200 to 1,000 years to form, but through overuse, lack of care or mistreatment, it can be swept off the land in just a few seasons. When soil is fertile, it is rich in *organic matter*, able to absorb water, and capable of producing abundant yields. Unfortunately, some natural events and some agricultural processes undermine the fertility of soil and threaten the *ecosystem* on which so much of life depends. Natural events, happenings not brought about through human intervention, frequently cause a loss of fertile soil. Strong winds can blow topsoil away, heavy rainfalls can wash it away, and protracted droughts can cause serious *depletion*. Agricultural experts tell us, however, that human mismanagement sometimes sets the stage for such phenomena to occur, and that some agricultural practices are direct causes of other forms of soil erosion.

State of the World 1989, a report commissioned by the Worldwatch Institute, contains the ominous warning that "much of the world's food production land is being sapped insidiously of its productive potential through overuse, lack of care, or unwise treatment, a process scientists call 'desertification.'"[4] The report continues:

> Each year, irreversible desertification claims an estimated 6 million *hectares* worldwide—a land area nearly twice the size of Belgium lost beyond practical hope of reclamation. An additional 20 million hectares annually become so impoverished that they are unprofitable to farm or graze. Most of the affected land, however, lies on the degradation continuum, somewhere between fully productive and hopelessly degraded. Unfortunately, much of it is sliding down the diminishing productivity side of the scale.[5]

Corrective or preventive measures need to be put in place in order to halt the process of land degradation. To this end agricultural experts advise that plowing of farmland be done on the contour, that is, at right angles to the slope of what is usually gently rolling land so as to keep the soil in place. Soil compaction, or the increased density of the soil, is caused by the repeated use of heavy farm machinery. When soil is compacted its ability to absorb water is decreased, causing its production capacity to decline. Less reliance on heavy machinery as well as changing the routes which such equipment follows can alleviate the problem of compaction. It is important to keep a plant cover or mulch on the earth during *fallow* periods in order to prevent soil from being blown or washed away. Intensivity of soil use, that is, attempting to have the soil repeatedly produce bumper crops year in and year out, leads to a loss of nutrients in the soil and its eventual ruin. Planning for fallow periods as well as less use of fertilizers can prevent the harm resulting from intensive agricultural production.

Monocropping can also lead to decreased agricultural production. According to Pierre R. Crosson and Norman J. Rosenberg,

> Since World War II there has been a worldwide trend away from crop rotation and toward continuous raising of a sin-

gle crop, such as corn. Monocropping can lead to sharp reductions in *genetic diversity*, with ominous results. A striking example occurred in the U.S. in 1970, when corn production was reduced 15 percent by a fungus well matched to the "T-cytoplasm" that had been incorporated in most of the hybrid seed corn planted in the U.S. corn belt. By the following year seed producers had stopped relying on T-cytoplasm, and a more variable genetic basis was established.[6]

Soil needs water in order to produce crops. Irrigation, however, is not without its difficulties. Seepage from canals and the over-watering of fields can cause the underlying *water table* to rise, resulting in water entering the root zone of crops and damaging them. In dry regions, *salinization* usually accompanies waterlogging as water near the surface of the earth evaporates, leaving behind a layer of salt that is toxic to plants.[7] Both root rotting and salinization point to the need for designing and implementing efficient irrigation and adequate drainage.

While pesticides and fertilizers bring many benefits to agriculture, Crosson and Rosenberg raise the following caution:

Pesticides and fertilizers are, along with irrigation and higher-yielding crop varieties, responsible for much of the remarkable increase in agricultural productivity that has taken place in the past few decades. But these substances can also have unfortunate side effects. Fertilizers and pesticides in *groundwater* may cause ailments ranging from cancer to methemoglobinemia (*"blue baby syndrome"*), which results from excess concentrations of nitrates in drinking water. Although good data are lacking, the rapid increase in the use of these agents around the world undoubtedly has some fairly serious health implications.[8]

Livestock feed on rangeland. If herds consume all the vegetation that grows on a given range, the barren earth which remains will be in danger of eroding. When there is a shortage of rangeland because of a drought, or there is an abundance of livestock because of overbreeding, it would make sense for ranchers to supplement a limited use of rangeland with purchased food for their herds. In this way they will insure the future of the rangeland.

In recent years tropical forests have frequently been cleared and converted into cropland or rangeland. Sandra Postel laments the conversion:

> Some portion of deforested land goes into sustainable land uses—such as traditional shifting cultivation, which includes a fallow period that restores the land's fertility—but the bulk of it does not. In the tropics today, deforestation usually translates into land degradation.[9]

Pollution of Soil from Toxic Waste

One of the lessons of recent history is that the ground on which we stand and the earth on which our food grows and our homes and schools and hospitals are built could have been contaminated because of improper disposal of toxic wastes. What are toxic wastes? How do toxic wastes come to pollute the soil? What harms might they cause humans? And what needs to be done in order to clean up toxic wastes?

A 1990 study by the Congressional Office of Technology Assessment reported that more than 65,000 toxic substances and chemicals are in use, and many pose potential hazards to human health.[10] In addition, there are also low level and high level radioactive wastes from nuclear power plants and from the nuclear weapons industry. Although we associate most hazardous wastes with industrial production and agriculture, many are found under the sink and in the garage. Examples include paints, thinners, pool chemicals, aerosol cans, toilet and drain cleaners, polishes and bleaches, waste oil and used gasoline.

Toxic wastes have come to pollute the soil in a number of ways. In Times Beach, Missouri a contractor who was hired by the town to spray roads for dust control in the 1970s did so with oil contaminated with *dioxin*. In 1983 the entire population of the town, 2,240 people, was evacuated because the area was judged unsalvageable.

Beginning in 1920 a partially completed channel between the upper and lower Niagara Rivers in upstate New York was used as a chemical dump by the Hooker Chemical Company. In 1953 the channel was filled in, and in the following years homes and schools were built on and around the site. In 1976 a consultant discovered toxic chemical residues in the air and sump pumps of many homes in the area. High levels of PCBs (*polychlorinated biphenyls*) were also found in the storm sewer system. The toxic chemicals dumped in the ground eventually necessitated the evacuation of all but 86 of the 900 families living in the region until such time as the land, water and buildings could be rendered safe for human habitation.[11]

A northern New Jersey factory which dumped radium used to make glow-in-the-dark watches at the turn of the century was the cause of serious contamination to 200 acres in three towns. More than 324,000 cubic yards of dirt, enough to fill 15,000 large dump trucks, will be removed in the cleanup; the cost to the federal government is estimated at $250 million.[12]

In view of the three examples just cited it is apparent that dumping hazardous chemicals directly into the ground, as well as applying them to the ground, causes pollution of the earth and makes the polluted areas temporarily or permanently uninhabitable. However, many instances of soil pollution have also occurred in spite of well-intentioned containerized disposal of toxic wastes. Problematic containers, which have either been buried in the ground or placed on top of the ground, have corroded with the passage of time, and their contents have leaked into or onto the earth, causing pollution.

Disposing of low level and high level *radioactive waste* from nuclear energy plants and the nuclear weapons industry is the most serious waste management issue facing society today. When this waste is placed in containers for disposal, there is fear that the containers will leak. Disposal in deserts and old mines is resisted by people who live in targeted states because they tend not to want to take even the slightest risk of exposure to radioactive substances. The tragedy at Chernobyl, while much greater than any soil contamination which could possibly follow leakage of comparably small amounts of radioactive waste into the earth, has undoubtedly intensified the widespread concern about radiation:

> The April 1986 explosion and fire at Chernobyl in the Soviet Union caused a partial meltdown of the plant's reactor core. More than seven tons of radioactive material were hurled into the atmosphere, eventually contaminating land, food, and water throughout much of Europe. Twenty-eight people died from acute radiation poisoning within 75 days of the accident, while another 300 were treated for serious radiation exposure. More than 100,000 people were evacuated from their homes, and up to 2,500 square *kilometers* became uninhabitable.[13]

Hazardous chemical wastes are capable of causing serious health problems. These range from relatively mild and transitory symptoms such as irritation to skin, eyes, nose and throat, dizziness, nausea and diarrhea to life-threatening cancers and damage to the nervous system, liver and kidneys. Fetal development can also be impaired and/or retarded by exposure to hazardous chemicals. The cells in the blood forming tissues, that is, bone marrow, the spleen and lymph nodes, are extremely sensitive to radiation and can be damaged if exposed to unsafe levels.

The United States Environmental Protection Agency is the entity charged with regulating and monitoring the disposal of toxic chemical wastes. The U.S. Department of Energy and the Pentagon work together with individual states on finding sites for radioactive waste disposal as well as ensuring that such waste is properly disposed of. In regard to toxic chemical wastes, the biggest contemporary problem entails cleaning up dump sites which were polluted as far back as the 1920s and identified only in recent years. A second task consists in enforcing those laws which are now on the books in order to prevent present-day pollution of the soil through chemical contamination.

It is estimated that there are 32,000 to 50,000 hazardous waste disposal sites throughout the United States. Of these, 1,000 to 2,000 are considered very dangerous. In 1980 the United States Congress passed a law to collect taxes so as to have the money to clean up these sites, and did in fact collect one billion dollars. Unfortunately, by 1985 only six chemical waste sites had been cleaned up; the rest of the money was spent on legal fees trying to determine which manufacturing and industrial firms bore responsibility for the costs of the cleanups.[14] It appears that the issue of cleaning up toxic dumps will be with us for the forseeable future. And it should be noted that wherever the contaminated soil from toxic dumps such as Love Canal and the radium-tainted areas of New Jersey is eventually placed becomes forever polluted soil which requires monitoring so as to prevent causing harm to humans and other life forms.

Depletion of the Earth's Resources

Since the Industrial Revolution the manufacturing and industrial sectors of the developed nations seem to have operated on the assumption that the earth's natural resources would always be there to be used. In recent years, however, it has become obvious that such resources as minerals, fossil fuels, and timber exist in limited quantities, and the necessity of setting limits in regard to their use is beginning to be recognized.

Minerals

In regard to the depletion of minerals, Robert D. Hamrin writes:

Until recently, minerals have been the "quiet" resource. One did not hear much about them. Yet industrial growth in the United States during this century has been dependent on a wide variety of high-quality mineral resources. In addition to minerals used for energy (coal, oil, gas, and uranium), about 100 other mineral commodities are consumed in agriculture, manufacturing, and other basic industries. Consumption of major nonfuel minerals increased in the first three post-World War II decades. While population increased 49 percent from 1948 to 1978, the consumption of ferrous metals increased 83 percent; phosphate rock, lime, and salt, 235 percent; and aluminum, 650 percent. More than 2 billion tons of nonfuel minerals were consumed in 1977 by the chemical, machinery, electrical, construction and transportation industries.[15]

As stocks of minerals dwindle, it becomes more difficult and costly to extract them from the earth. A temporary solution is to turn to other nations and to import needed minerals from them. In time, however, if demand continues, these sources of minerals will also become depleted. Ultimately, it will be necessary to accept the fact that minerals do not regenerate and to develop industrial plans which contain less reliance on minerals and which call for more industrial use of recycled minerals or mineral substitutes.

Fossil Fuels

Most of the fuels used by industrialized nations are in the form of incompletely oxidized and decayed animal and vegetable materials known as fossil fuels. Coal, peat, lignite, petroleum and natural gas are fossil fuels; they are used—frequently by burning—to provide heat and energy. As with minerals, the earth's supply of fossil fuels has been significantly depleted during the past few generations, and there are projections that these fuels may be exhausted in the years ahead. Should an *exponentially rising rate of depletion* occur, estimated world resources of coal would be depleted in about one hundred years, resources of oil would be exhausted in about forty years, and reserves of natural gas might last only thirty years.[16]

Only by significant reduction in reliance on fossil fuels and development of alternative energy sources can our First World technological society continue on its present course. Using less fossil fuels more efficiently as well as harnessing energy from the sun, the waters and the wind are suggested as possible long-term solutions to depletion of the earth's store of fossil fuels. Turning to nuclear energy, which relies on energy stored in the atom and released through fission, fusion or radioactivity for its power, tends to meet with widespread resistance because of the risk of nuclear accidents (such as at *Three Mile Island*) and problems associated with disposal of nuclear waste.

Timber

Just as fossil fuels and minerals are a resource of the land, so, too, are trees. Like a mineral which is extracted from the earth or oil which is pumped from a well, when a tree is cut down it is gone forever. However, if a new tree is planted to replace each tree which is cut down, forests can regenerate and the number of trees will remain stable. This is not to say that saplings are equivalent to beautiful (some would say "venerable") trees which are hundreds of years old, but only to state that replacement of trees is possible. In reality, over the past several hundred years there has been a significant decrease in the earth's forests, and only fairly recently have programs been instituted to plant new trees to replace those which are cut down. Robert D. Hamrin's historical survey of the dimishing amount of U.S. forestland and the amount of timber available for commercial use provide an interesting overview:

> When Europeans first came to the New World, about 950 million acres of what became the United Sates was covered with trees. Of this, about 90 percent was "commercially productive" by today's standards. Today that forested acreage has shrunk to 740 million acres, and only 65 percent of it is commercially productive. Moreover, the U.S. Forest Service projects that if current trends continue, demand for wood from U.S. forests is likely to surpass supplies by 1990.[17]

In cutting down trees the character of a particular locale is significantly altered and a valuable natural resource, which may take hundreds of years to replace, is depleted. In addition, *habitat* destruction accompanies extensive forest clearing. In view of this fact, at this writing, an environmental movement to save the spotted owl, which lives in the forests of northern California, Oregon and Washington, is underway.[18] Opposition to the movement is forthcoming from loggers, truck drivers and sawmill workers whose livelihoods depend on acquiring timber from these forests. Regardless of the way in which this particular issue is resolved, nothing will change in respect to the thousands of other species which became extinct in the past because no effective action was taken to preserve their habitats.

Loss of Tropical Rain Forests

Tropical rain forests are among the most species-rich habitats on earth. The enormous biological diversity found in these forests can be explained by the fact that the most species-rich groups on earth, the *invertebrates* and flowering plants, are concentrated there. The vegetation, much of it broad-leaved evergreens, is extremely lush; the tallest trees tower as much as 100 feet above the rain forest floor.[19] At the present time, rain forests in nine countries are threatened by plans for clear-cutting; these countries are Brazil, Indonesia, Vietnam, Thailand, the Philippines, Costa Rica, Cameroon, and Myanmar (formerly Burma).[20]

Scientists and environmentally conscious citizens are objecting to the loss of tropical forests which each year is estimated at 40 to 50 million acres worldwide, an area the size of Washington State.[21] One of the principal reasons for the objection is that at least half the species on earth live in moist tropical forests,[22] and, if their habitats are destroyed, they will be threatened with extinction. (The other reason concerns global warming and will be treated below.) Edward O. Wilson provides a description of the connection between rain forest clearing and species extinction:

> I have conservatively estimated that on a worldwide basis the ultimate loss attributable to rain forest clearing alone (at the present 1 percent rate) is from .2 to .3 percent of all species in the forests per year. Taking a very conservative figure of two million species confined to the forests, the global loss that results from deforestation could be as much as from 4,000 to 6,000 species a year. That in turn is on the order of 10,000 times greater than the naturally occurring background extinction rate that existed prior to the appearance of human beings.[23]

At least five known negative consequences would attend such a significant reduction of species. The first is that scientists will lose forever the possibility of learning about the genetic codes of extinct species. Without species diversity it will be more difficult for those fewer species which remain to adapt to changed habitats, thus further lessening the total number of species. As yet undiscovered crop species which could become food for humans will pass from the scene as will wild plant and animal species which are potential sources of fiber and petroleum substitutes. In this connection, Donald A. Falk asserts:

> It is the diversity of species—and *only* that—that will permit our forests, grasslands and deserts to adapt to a changing global climate. If world agriculture is to feed 10 billion people less than 40 years from now, we will need every living adaptation we can find for growing plants in poor soil and with low rainfall.[24]

Finally, such inconspicuous plants as the rosy periwinkle which is the source of *vinblastine* and *vincristine*, two *alkaloids* which are effective against Hodgkin's disease and acute lymphocytic leukemia, may also be lost.[25] It would be unrealistic to expect the earth to quickly regenerate new species to replace those which are lost because such a process is estimated to last between five and ten million years.[26]

Rain forest clearing is generally undertaken in order to acquire croplands or rangelands. Ironically, tropical forests usually have infertile soil because most of the nutrients are in the vegetation, not the soil, and, after only a few years of use, farmers and ranchers wind up abandoning the land.[27] In view of the ultimate futility of converting rain forests to agricultural purposes and all the other negative consequences which attend thereto, there is widespread resistance to the loss of these forests. The World Resources Institute, an international research group, in collaboration with the United Nations Environment and Development Programs, has consequently recommended that clear cutting be halted so as to prevent further environmental degradation.[28]

Garbage—Landfill—Recycling—And Beyond

The United States recycles only 10 percent of the 160 million tons of trash it creates each year.[29] Producing garbage goes hand-in-hand with an affluent lifestyle. Industrial processes generate a large volume of waste which has, up until relatively recently, been taken for granted as an inherent aspect of production. In addition, consumers have steadily increased the volume of solid waste, and only in the past decade have they begun to have second thoughts about throwaways and disposables and the overall amount of trash coming from their homes.

Disposal of solid waste is beginning to be seen as a significant environmental problem. People are realizing that they are generating waste which is hard to dispose of while at the same time exhausting such natural resources as timber and minerals. Two reasons for the current scarcity of landfill space are the sheer volume of trash to be disposed of and the *nonbiodegradability* of the plastics and styrofoam which comprise such a large part of today's garbage. Plastic and styrofoam objects take up a significant amount of landfill space and items dumped today will be there—unchanged—hundreds of years from now.

Environmental regulations and citizen objections are making it more difficult to open new landfills. New landfills are more costly now than in the past. Regulations require that landfills be lined in order to prevent leakage of hazardous substances sometimes found in household garbage into nearby *groundwater*. With existing landfills nearing capacity, new landfills tend to be located further and further from populated areas, necessitating the transport of garbage over long distances. Wherever a garbage dump is located, it pollutes the soil, is unattractive and is the source of unpleasant odors. Consequently, residents are likely to oppose the establishment of dumps in their locales, and the presence of a dump in any undeveloped area constitutes a disincentive to development of that area.

It is becoming apparent that there are several answers to the garbage crisis. The most obvious is that overall waste generation needs to be reduced. Industrial research and development personnel are starting to figure out how residues from one process can become raw materials for others. The theory of planned obsolescence, an approach to manufactured items according to which such goods as automobiles and appliances are made with a short lifespan in view, is beginning to be rethought. Cars, televisions and refrigerators take up a lot of landfill space and their production requires the use of scarce natural resources; it would make more environmental sense (and, in the long run, might make more economic sense) to build these items to last.

Consumers are becoming aware of the problematic aspects of styrofoam and plastic. They are also adopting new behaviors. For example, carrying cloth tote bags for purchases instead of using paper or plastic bags provided by merchants is a simple and effective strategy for cutting down on the amount of waste. Re-using cloth napkins, cloth diapers and other items such as drinking glasses and coffee mugs, rather than depending on disposable substitutes, is another way to decrease solid waste. Turning kitchen scraps and garden clippings into compost is also an excellent strategy for reducing garbage and an *organic way* to build up the nutrients in the garden. The most significant difference in trash reduction, however, can be made through recycling.

Recycling means reusing trash. It entails the division of trash into several categories. Newspaper, glass separated according to color, aluminum and tin cans, and some kinds of plastic can be recycled. In states which have adopted mandatory recycling laws, huge amounts of recyclable material have been recovered, thus lessening dependence on scarce natural resources while not further impinging on available landfill space. A goal of recycling 40 to 50 percent of household trash, while ambitious, would not be impossible to achieve and would lessen the mess constituted by garbage.

The Atmosphere Is Endangered

Air Pollution

We walk on the earth and we breathe the air which surrounds us. The sometimes transparent and sometimes discolored air which fills the void between the earth's floor and the sky's ceiling is known as the atmosphere. The lower 10 to 15 *kilometers* of the atmosphere is called the troposphere. Accordingly, we breathe the air of the lower troposphere. The stratosphere is the other portion of the atmosphere; it extends from roughly 10 kilometers to approximately 50 kilometers above the surface of the earth. The closest we ordinarily come to contact with the stratosphere is during air travel when we look out the windows of a plane. As we shall see, the whole of the atmosphere is endangered. However, we shall begin our survey of threats to the atmosphere by considering the phenomenon called air pollution.

Just as toxic substances harm the soil, so, too, toxic substances pollute the air. Particulates—which are solid particles or liquid droplets small enough to remain suspended in air[30] primarily come into the air as a result of coal burning, incineration or industrial processes. Particulates contain high concentrations of sulfur dioxide which is a major contributor to respiratory diseases in humans. Nitrogen dioxide which comes from power plants and motor vehicles, also causes respiratory disease. Carbon monoxide, which comes from motor vehicles, interferes with the absorption of oxygen by red blood cells, thereby slowing reflexes, causing drowsiness and weakening judgment.[31] Hydrocarbons result from chains of atoms linked with each other and hydrogen atoms. They are present in engine exhaust and are created by the incomplete burning of fuels.[32] Although they are but one of the ingredients of smog, they are partially responsible for its deleterious effects. If inhaled or ingested, asbestos, a building material, is extremely harmful to human health. When, in the process of removing asbestos from a building, it is broken up and becomes airborne, it constitutes a toxic air pollutant and a significant health hazard.[33] So, too, do literally thousands of workplace chemicals which, if incorrectly handled, might come to pollute the air. A partial list compiled from the New Jersey Department of Health Hazardous Substance Fact Sheet terms the following airborne chemicals especially dangerous in the workplace, but does not provide specific data when they are diluted in the air beyond the plant:

Acetone: High concentrations can cause dizziness and lack of consciousness. Can irritate the skin, eyes, nose and throat.

Ethylene glycol: Can irritate the eyes, nose and throat. Can cause nausea, vomiting and headaches. May cause birth defects. Repeated or high exposure can cause kidney damage or stones. Brain damage may also occur.

Hydrochloric acid: Can irritate the lungs, and higher exposure can cause a fatal buildup in the lungs.

Methanol: Irritates the eyes, nose, mouth and throat. Can cause liver damage.

Sodium hydroxide: Breathing the dust or droplets can irritate and burn the lungs.

Xylene: Can irritate the eyes, nose and throat; high levels can cause loss of consciousness and death. May damage fetuses. Repeated exposure may damage bone marrow, eyes and cause stomach problems.[34]

According to Cynthia Pollock Shea, "Ozone, the same compound that acts as a protective shield in the stratosphere, is a noxious pollutant at ground level."[35] The main component of smog, the dirty, brownish air that often blankets urban areas and sometimes even travels to unpopulated areas, ozone retards crop and tree growth, limits visibility and impairs respiratory function. Over time, it also causes the facades of buildings to crumble.[36] Shea writes that "Doctors now warn that everyone, not just people with impaired respiratory functions, is threatened."[37]

Among the causes of today's polluted air are fires (including wood burning stoves), oil and gas production, chemicals released by solvents, paints and coatings, and waste treatment by incineration. In regard to the problem of the decreased amount of landfill space for garbage, incineration of trash may appear to be a reasonable alternative until we realize that the soot and noxious particles which result from burning garbage contribute significantly to air pollution. The fact that incinerators can cause up to $500 million to construct is a further disincentive to considering them a solution to the solid waste crisis.

All the above mentioned causes of air pollution pale, however, in comparison to the amount of pollution caused by motor vehicles. Close to 400 million vehicles clog the world's streets today,[38] up from 195 million in 1970 and 321 million in 1980.[39] Michael Renner contends that "Cars, trucks, and buses play a prominent role in generating virtually all the major air pollutants, especially in cities."[40] He says that, in nations which belong to the *Organization for Economic Cooperation and Development* (OECD), motor vehicles contribute 75 percent of carbon monoxide emissions, 48 percent of nitrogen oxides, 40 percent of hydrocarbons, 13 percent of particulates, and 3 percent of sulfur oxides.[41]

Possible ways to deal with the pollution caused by motor vehicles include developing cleaner fuels and requiring proper maintenance of catalytic converters. Such cleaner fuels as methanol, ethanol, natural gas, hydrogen and electricity are being studied as alternatives to gasoline. Although some of these fuels have significant drawbacks (e.g., natural gas has an explosive potential), at the present time research and development efforts are aimed at determining the circumstances under which their use might be feasible and less harmful overall than gasoline. The catalytic converter is a recent emission control device which, if properly maintained, is capable of cutting emissions of hydrocarbons by an average of 87 percent, of carbon monoxide by 85 percent, and of nitrogen oxides by 62 percent.[42] Technology needs to address the fact that catalytic converters are least effective when engines are cold, and society needs to decide what action to take in regard to older motor vehicles which were built without catalytic converters. Ultimately, the fact that the catalytic converter is only capable of lessening (but not eliminating) noxious emissions must also be faced, along with the vast amount of pollution generated within even the best possible scenario.

Acid Rain

Two invisible gases, sulfur dioxide and nitrogen oxide, have been released into the atmosphere in increasing quantities during the past several decades. Sulfur dioxide is released when coal is burned, and nitrogen oxide is one of the gases which comes from automobile tailpipes. The quantity is much greater in vehicles which lack a catalytic converter. Sulfur dioxide and nitrogen oxide can remain close to the sites from which they are discharged, or these gases can be carried by the wind for hundreds or even thousands of miles. En route through the atmosphere these pollutant molecules interact with sunlight, moisture, *oxidants* and *catalysts* in order to change into new, acid-laden compounds of sulfur and nitrogen.[43] When these acid-laden compounds are incorporated into rain, snow, drizzle, fog, frost and dew, such precipitation is called acid rain.

According to Will Steger and Jon Bowermaster, precipitation is categorized as acid rain by employing the process of measurement which they describe:

> "Potential of hydrogen"—or pH—is the measure used to determine a substance's acidity. The scale runs from 1 to 14 (and can be estimated by anyone using litmus paper and a measuring scale bought at your local drugstore . . .). The more acid a substance, the lower the number: natural rainfall averages between pH 5.0 and 5.6; Coca-cola has a pH value of 4; vinegar, 2.2; and battery acid has a pH of 1. A pH value of 4 is *10 times* more acidic than 5. Acid rain has a pH of less than 5.[44]

Acid rain causes many harmful consequences; Robert Hamrin summarizes them as follows:

> In Scandinavia, southern Canada, and the northeastern part of the United States, many lakes and *estuaries* have experienced depletion of fish life, and in some cases, they have become totally devoid of fish. Such losses are an indication of major upsets in ecological balances, which may be more far-reaching than the recreational resource loss. In addition, loss of crop productivity and forest yields due to acid rain may be prevalent. Acid rain also damages steel and stone structures as well as works of art. Many of these effects may be permanent.[45]

In 1984 West Germany reported that more than half of its forests were damaged by acid rain. As of 1990, the Black Forest of Bavaria had lost one-third of its trees, and damage to the country's timber industry is estimated at $800 million per year.[46] The continuing presence of acid rain, together with the fact that it has polluted the soil of the forest, discourages expectations for regrowth. In regard to lakes, acid rain affects them by altering their fundamental ecology. When acid concentration builds up, plant and animal life shrivels. Some lakes may be able to restore themselves if acid input can be halted or treated through the addition of lime, but, if sufficiently weakened by acid and other pollutants, the lakes' natural recovery mechanism may be permanently destroyed.

In order to deal effectively with acid rain, a concerted effort to lessen the amount of gases which cause it needs to be put in place. Since, as we have seen, catalytic converters reduce the amount of nitrogen oxide from auto emissions by 62%, their immediate worldwide use would be a significant step in the right direction. (At present, catalytic converters are only required by law for automobiles purchased in the United States.) In regard to reducing sulfur dioxide emissions from smokestacks, the use of *scrubbers* to clean sulfur from smoke and gas, or using low sulfur coal are recommended. Industrial leaders are also suppporting research and testing of "clean coal technologies" which aim at controlling pollution in the combustion process rather than employing scrubbers which are an expensive way of cleaning up.[47]

Climate Change: The Greenhouse Effect or Global Warming

In the years following the Industrial Revolution the amount of carbon dioxide in the atmosphere has increased by approximately 25 percent. Increased carbon dioxide is a result of the burning of fossil fuels accompanied by a decrease in the number of trees by deforestation. (Trees take in carbon dioxide to use in the process of photosynthesis.) Carbon dioxide, in combination with methane, chloroflourocarbons, oxides of nitrogen and low level ozone, is said to produce a greenhouse-like cover above the earth's atmosphere. Just as the glass of a greenhouse allows sunlight to stream in but keeps the sun's heat inside, so does the shield formed by greenhouse gases keep the sun's heat, along with the heat the earth generates, close to the earth. This phenomenon is said to raise the earth's temperature and is called global warming.

Scientists project that the atmospheric concentration of carbon dioxide will reach 600 parts per million, or about twice the level of 1900, sometime between 2030 and 2080.[48] If these projections are

accurate, the earth's temperature could conceivably go up between
3.0 and 5.5 Celsius, a change unprecedented in human history. It
would match the five degree warming since the peak of the last ice
age 18,000 years ago but would take effect between 10 and 100
times faster.[49]

If the earth is indeed warming as a result of the shield con-
structed by carbon dioxide and other gases, what environmental
consequences are in store for us? Scientists see global warming as
presenting threats to natural ecosystems. Will Steger and Jon
Bowermaster speculate:

> Many forests would turn to grasslands, water supplies
> would be tainted, recreational lakes would dry up, wet-
> lands would flood. Higher water temperatures and rising
> sea levels would reduce fish and shellfish populations . . .
> Fifty to 90 percent of America's salt marshes, swamps, and
> bayous—some of the most diverse natural habitats—would
> be destroyed. Devastating changes might occur in the
> oceans, which would be affected in ways no one can rea-
> sonably predict.[50]

Agricultural production would also be significantly affected by
global warming. Stephen H. Schneider, relying on studies prepared by the late Dean F. Peterson, Jr. of Utah State University and
Andrew Keller of Keller-Bliesner Engineering in Logan, Utah, suggests that a three degree warming combined with a 10 percent
drop in precipitation would result in one-third less viable acreage
in arid regions of the western states and the Great Plains.[51] (A
decline in summer precipitation is a predicted concomitant of
global warming.)

The habitability of coastal areas and the availability of sufficient
supplies of potable drinking water is expected to be detrimentally
affected by global warming. In this regard, Lester R. Brown, Christopher Flavin and Sandra Postel write:

> In the United States, a U.S. government-sponsored study
> has estimated the potential impacts of climate change on
> Cleveland, Miami, and New York. A few minor benefits
> are mentioned, such as lower snow removal budgets and

winter heating bills, but the overall picture is bleak. In particular, many billions of dollars will likely have to be spent on improving already inadequate water supply systems, since demand will increase and supplies will be degraded as the climate changes.

In New York, for example, salt water could move up the lower Hudson River while more severe droughts limit the amount of water available from upstate watersheds. In Miami, most of which was once below sea-level, even extensive diking will not preserve its porous freshwater aquifer. If global warming continues, Miami could one day be reclaimed by the sea.[52]

The two biggest questions about global warming are whether or not the predictions will come to pass, and, if they have merit, what ought to be done about the situation. Projections about global warming are based on mathematical computer models which have some shortcomings. Stephen Schneider admits that such climatically important processes as atmospheric turbulence, precipitation and cloud formation cannot be simulated directly, and thus are subject to the programmer's calculations. In addition, the way in which clouds interact with other atmospheric agents is often overlooked, and the dynamics of the oceans' impact on weather tends to be oversimplified.[53] These drawbacks notwithstanding, Schneider contends:

the models are well enough validated and other evidence of greenhouse-gas effects on climate is strong enough, so that most of us (climatologists) believe that the increases in average surface temperature predicted by the models for the next 50 years or so are probably valid within a rough factor of two. (By "probably" I mean it is a better than even bet.) Within a decade or so, warming of the predicted magnitude should be clearly evident.[54]

The second question asks, given the predictions of global warming, what ought to be done now. The choices which humankind has are to act promptly to reduce levels of carbon dioxide and the other gases which cause global warming, or to wait and see what happens, being prepared to adapt to whatever changes take place in the years ahead. Since responding to this question ultimately entails value judgments, it will be addressed in subsequent chapters.

Depletion of the Ozone Layer

Ozone is a toxic chemical when close to the earth's surface, but in the stratosphere it performs the necessary and beneficial function of blocking the sun's ultraviolet light. Without an intact ozone layer to absorb much of the ultraviolet radiation emitted by the sun, scientists say that humans will be at risk of increased incidence of skin cancer, cataracts and suppression of the immune system. Harms to wildlife, crops, terrestrial and aquatic ecosystems are also predicted.[55]

In 1974 scientists at the University of California at Irvine predicted a decline in global ozone, but the international scientific community was sceptical. In 1985, a team led by Joseph Farman, of the British Antarctic Survey, startled the world by reporting a 40 percent loss in the springtime ozone layer over Antarctica—a hole that was later described as larger than the United States and taller than Mount Everest.[56] Although the scientific community is not in unanimous agreement that ozone depletion has occurred in areas other than Antarctica and that ozone depletion represents a significant threat to the planet, a substantial number of atmospheric scientists have come to hold this position. Cynthia Pollock Shea points to the release of a NASA report as the occasion for the articulation of the growing consensus:

> A greater understanding of and consensus about ozone depletion was made possible by the release of the NASA Ozone Trends Panel report on March 15, 1988. More than 100 scientists from 10 countries spent 16 months reviewing the published literature and performing a critical reanalysis and interpretation of nearly all ground-based and satellite-derived ozone data. Their purpose: to eliminate any errors caused by improperly calibrated instruments.

Ozone losses were documented around the globe, not just at the poles; the blame, particularly for the Antarctic ozone hole, was firmly placed on chlorofluorocarbons. The panel reported that between 30 and 60 degrees north, where most of the world's people live, total-column ozone had increased by 1.7 - 3.0 percent between 1969 and 1986. Further, "ozone decreases were most pronounced in winter, ranging from 2.3 - 6.2 percent (depending on latitude), and those winter changes were higher than predicted by atmospheric models."

. . . The report further stated that while the problem was worst over Antarctica during the spring, "ozone appears to have decreased since 1979 by 5 percent or more at all latitudes south of 60 degrees south throughout the year." The hole alone covers approximately 10 percent of the southern hemisphere.[57]

Ozone depletion is caused principally by chlorofluorocarbons (CFCs) and halons—human made chemicals which make their way into the stratosphere. Chlorofluorocarbons are used to provide the cooling in air conditioning and refrigeration as well as in aerosol sprays and in the production of rigid foam insulation and flexible foam such as styrofoam. Halons are a chemical used to fight fires; they can be applied directly to sensitive equipment without causing damage or leaving a residue. When the chlorine from CFCs and the bromine from halons reach the stratosphere they break apart the ozone molecules which make up the ozone layer. Scientists tell us that the chlorine in one CFC molecule can destroy thousands of ozone molecules before it breaks up and gets washed from the atmosphere.   They also contend that even if CFC emissions were halted immediately the destruction of stratospheric ozone would continue for at least a century.[58] The bromine in halons is even more effective in destroying ozone than chlorine; however, there is far less bromine in the stratosphere.

In recent years some people have argued that "if all known technical control measures were used, total CFC and halon emissions could be reduced by approximately 90 percent," and that control of emissions, not abandoning the chemicals, is the logical approach to take.[59]   Others, arguing that there is an urgent need to halt all use of CFCs and halons, and to direct research to the speedy development of environmentally suitable alternatives, have prevailed over those who advocate control measures.   On June 29, 1990 ninety-three nations agreed to halt the production of chemicals that destroy the ozone layer by the year 2000.   We can only hope that this measure has been taken in time.

The Waters Are Endangered

Ocean Pollution

Will Steger and Jon Bowermaster remind us of the significance of the ocean:

> Life began in the ocean more than 3.5 billion years ago; fossils of sea life predate those of land creatures. Salt water covers 71 percent of the globe, comprises 97 percent of all the water on Earth and contains over 80 percent of all living matter. It warehouses and distributes the sun's energy, serving as a kind of global thermostat which helps regulate the world's climate.[60]

If it goes without saying that oceans are important, it is likewise true that they have been endangered as a result of human activity. What humans intentionally dump into oceans, as well as accidental oil spills, have accounted for ecological problems. Let us consider first what is dumped into the oceans.

Not all garbage is disposed of in land fills, by incineration or through recycling. Fishing vessels toss more than 340,000 tons of garbage into the seas yearly, and cruise ships and navies add another million pounds of waste a day.[61]   A total of 14 billion pounds of garbage, sewage and sludge generated on land is also dumped into the oceans each year. In 1988 media coverage of medical waste washing up on beaches along the east coast of the United States made people aware of illegal offshore disposal of wastes in contempt of government regulations forbidding such activity.

The sheer volume of trash which is dumped presents a challenge for oceans which have been considered capable of absorbing and decomposing it. Both sludge, which is treated sewage, and untreated sewage are dumped into oceans, piped into oceans, or, after heavy rains, carried as runoff into the oceans. Even when properly treated, sewage waste water contains enough pollutants—bacteria, nitrogen and phosphorus—to reduce ocean oxygen levels and suffocate marine life.

Just as chemicals used in association with industrial production find their way into the soil and the air, so, too, some wind up on the ocean's floor. DDT, a powerful and toxic insecticide and PCBs (polychlorinated biphenyls, a group of toxic chemicals that were long used in industry and that take the form of a thick, odorless liquid), as well as heavy metal compounds such as lead, cadmium and mercury, have already spread throughout the world's marine ecosystems, in part through gradual accumulation in the food chain.[62] The food chain is contaminated as toxic chemicals and metals are ingested by small organisms which live on the ocean floor; these small organisms are subsequently eaten by fish and shellfish which then become bearers of toxins. Considering that consumption of fish and shellfish has reached 14.5 pounds per person per year in the United States,[63] contamination of the aquatic food chain is a cause for concern.

The dumping of plastics into the oceans presents harmful threats directly to marine life. In this connection, Steger and Bowermaster write:

> Many consider plastics the most devastating manmade threat facing the ocean. The U.S. Office of Technology Assessment concludes that plastic pollution is a greater threat to marine mammals and birds than are pesticides, oil spills, or contaminated runoff. It credits plastic with killing more than one million birds and tens of thousands of seals, sea lions, sea otters, whales, dolphins, porpoises and turtles annually. Because plastic is often transparent, it nets or entwines animals that cannot see it. It floats on waves and can be easily mistaken for food. Animals surface stuck in

six-pack holders or wash up on beaches, their stomachs swollen by garbage bags they've swallowed.[64]

An estuary is a place where the inflowing freshwater of rivers meets and mixes with saltwater in coastal bays and inlets. Estuaries are among the most productive marine ecosystems because the eggs of many fish and *crustacean* species are laid in these ecosystems and many marine organisms pass their early stages in estuaries. Ocean pollution, or direct pollution of estuaries themselves from runoff or adjacent development, results in contamination of fish and shellfish in their breeding grounds. In addition, pollution of estuaries can also result in the propagation of large numbers of red and brown algae which feed on the nitrates and phosphates found in pollutants. These algae cover wide swaths of bays and inlets, absorbing life-sustaining oxygen from the water and thus endangering marine life. As the algae die they continue suffocating other life forms by settling to the bottom of the estuary.

Since 1967 there have been four major oil spills and dozens of smaller ones. In 1967, the *Torrey Canyon* ran aground off Sicily, spilling 37 million gallons. In 1978, the *Amoco Cadiz* spilled more than 68 million gallons of oil off the coast of France. In 1979, the *Atlantic Empress* spilled 45 million gallons into the seas off Trinidad. Perhaps the most famous oil spill involved the *Exxon Valdez* when, in 1989, 11 million gallons of thick black crude oil spilled from a hole in its hull into Prince William Sound off the coast of Alaska. Oil in oceans makes them uninhabitable to most forms of life. In addition to poisoning the waters, tar balls are carried by currents to nearby beaches where they foul these recreational areas.

While it is clear that oceans are endangered, scientists theorize that the damage which has been done can be reversed. By banning the dumping of toxic wastes, radioactive wastes and plastics, by adequately treating all sewage before it is discharged, and by monitoring communities located near estuaries, much of the harm to spawning grounds and oceans can be eliminated or reduced. Since it is impossible to clean up or contain oil spills in excess of 100,000 gallons, strict preventive measures need to be put in place in order to avoid future oil spills.

Freshwater Pollution

Oceans contain salt water; sources of non-salt water fall within the category "freshwater." Snow, rain, ice, rivers, springs, lakes, ponds, streams, wetlands and groundwater aquifers are all forms of freshwater. There are approximately 9,000 cubic kilometers of freshwater available for use each year throughout the world; this amount is sufficient to meet the requirements of 20 billion people.[65] Since sources of freshwater are unevenly distributed, however, supplies are generally more available in developed countries while tending to be scarce in undeveloped countries.[66] Large quantities of freshwater are used in agriculture; lesser amounts are used by humans for drinking, food preparation, bathing, laundering, flushing and other domestic uses. Animals, birds and vegetation also depend on freshwater for survival.

Unfortunately, many sources of freshwater are polluted. Will Steger and Jon Bowermaster, commenting on the fact that people in the United States are not inclined to raise questions about the quality of the water coming from the tap, suggest some reasons for concern:

> . . . before it gushes from the kitchen tap (water) may have helped to irrigate farmland and picked up herbicides, pesticides, and fertilizers along the way. It may also include remnants of the runoff from nearby streets that is laden with oil, grease, cadmium, and lead. While the water from your tap may have begun as an icy mountain spring, it may also have passed beneath a chemical company's discharge pipe. Hazardous waste injected deep into the ground may have spread to your groundwater source, or your water may be tainted by substances leaching from nearby landfills.[67]

In the United States water used for domestic, industrial and agricultural purposes generally comes from reservoirs or from groundwater aquifers. Water from rain, melted snow and ice, runoff and water from springs is collected in a reservoir and piped to the communities served by the reservoir. Groundwater aquifers are found beneath the surface of the earth. Aquifers fill the open space within long stretches of porous rock, sand or gravel, and they contain soil materials as well as rocks such as sandstone. Water is obtained from groundwater aquifers through the use of wells from which it is pumped to the surface of the earth. Whether stored in reservoirs or procured from aquifers, in developed nations freshwater is treated by filtration and disinfection before it is piped to the communities which use it. These processes, however, as noted by Steger and Bowermaster, may not be completely successful in removing all pollutants. In underdeveloped countries freshwater is not always adequately treated and can be the medium for transmitting many serious diseases. The most serious disease is diarrhea which kills 1,000 children in the world every hour.[68] Other waterborne diseases include hepatitis, malaria, typhoid, cholera, leprosy and yellow fever.[69]

In the United States water in aquifers can be contaminated by toxins from pesticides, herbicides and industrial processes. Through a process known as leaching they can seep into aquifers through the soil or drip directly into the groundwater. Oil and gas tanks, as well as containerized toxic wastes can contaminate groundwater through gradual leakage. In addition, the lead and solder from corroded pipes can penetrate into and pollute groundwater. There is no technology available to restore aquifers once they have been polluted, and, therefore, after contamination polluted groundwater is no longer suitable for use.

Between pollution of some sources of groundwater and shrinkage of groundwater in some areas, continued availability of adequate supplies of fresh water should not be taken for granted. In the United States water tables are falling from 6 inches to 4 feet per year beneath one-fourth of the irrigated cropland.[70] The reason for the falling water tables is either because pumping is exceeding the rate of aquifer recharge or because the water is from the largely nonrenewable Ogallala Aquifer.[71] The Ogallala Aquifer underlies parts of Texas, New Mexico, Oklahoma, Colorado, Kansas and Nebraska—one of the most important agricultural regions of the United States. If water depletion continues at its present rate, in the not too distant future residents of this area may have to look beyond their boundaries for the water they require.[72]

Rivers, lakes, streams, springs, ponds and wetlands contain freshwater and are habitats for diverse and important ecosystems. In recent years rivers and lakes have been polluted by receiving more sewage than they are capable of biodegrading. Toxins have entered rivers and lakes as well as streams, springs and ponds from runoff, acid rain and from direct dumping. Some chemicals, such as the PCBs found in the Hudson River, have found their way to river bottoms and formed a slimy sludge. After being located and identified, disposal of sludge becomes a major problem because no community is willing to accept it, regardless of the number of precautions which go into the design of the landfill. In addition to many harrowing stories of freshwater pollution, the environmental literature also contains accounts of the restoration of rivers and lakes which has been accomplished through enforcing regulations aimed at polluters. Recovering systems such as the Cuyahoga River in Ohio and Lake Erie, one of the largest lakes in North America, provide proof that with time and determination the effects of pollution can be reversed. It is apparent, however, that the future of earth's freshwater resources is much more closely connected to prevention of pollution than to measures initiated after the fact. In addition, if the possibility of global warming becomes a reality, sources of freshwater located near the coastline would be in danger of being overrun by salt water, and would then no longer be able to serve the functions attributed to freshwater. Within such a scenario, today's serious situation would become a full-scale crisis.

Conclusion

The foregoing establishes the fact that the earth is endangered in many ways. The interrelatedness of the harms which threaten the earth and the fact that many pollutants cross borders unchecked should be apparent. The truth is that most of the dangers to the earth's environment are the result of unwise human action. Learning the status of the earth's degradation to date and keeping up with environmental news are the essential prerequisites for what should follow: a well thought out and properly motivated plan for restoring the well-being of the planet.

Exercise

On April 22, 1990, Senator Al Gore, Jr. of Tennessee wrote an op-ed piece in *The New York Times* on the subject of global warming. Consider the following question and answer:

> *Q*. Aren't the dire predictions about global warming based on unreliable computer models? How do we know that there is any correlation between increased levels of carbon dioxide in the atmosphere and changes in temperature?
>
> *A*. The most compelling evidence comes from careful studies of tiny air bubbles in Antarctic ice. These show what has actually happened to the Earth's climate during the last 160,000 years. . . . Carbon dioxide and temperature have gone up and down in lockstep for as far back as scientists can measure.
>
> Through the last two ice ages and the period of great warming in between, levels of carbon dioxide have fluctuated between 200 and 300 parts per million. Even the sceptics agree that concentrations of carbon dioxide will be pushed to levels of 600 parts per million within the next 35 to 45 years. It is irresponsible to assume that after moving in tandem with carbon dioxide for 160,000 years, temperatures will not be affected by these dramatic increases.[73]

Sherwood B. Idso, a research physicist at the Department of Agriculture Water Conservation Laboratory in Phoenix, Arizona responded to Senator Gore in a letter to the Editor which was published on April 24, 1990. Among other things, Mr. Idso contested Gore's citation of data regarding the ice core and wrote:

> . . . changes in carbon dioxide concentration cannot be claimed to be the cause of changes in air temperature because the appropriate sequence of events (temperature changes following carbon dioxide change) is not only never present in the data, but it is actually violated in half of the record.[74]

Idso goes on to say that increased carbon dioxide in the air will be a boon to plants. He said that it will reduce "the rate at which water is lost to the atmosphere through individual plant leaves, greatly increasing the efficiency with which plants use water in producing organic matter. Plants of the future will be able to grow in areas that have been too dry for them."[75]

Raymond D. Clarke, Professor of Biology at Sarah Lawrence College and George M. Woodwell, Director, Woods Hole Research Center in Woods Hole, Massachusetts subsequently responded to Sherwood B. Idso. Clarke attacked Idso's "unsubstantiated conjecture" about increased carbon dioxide in the air and benefits to plant life as well as what he perceived to be a "simplistic way of thinking."[76]

Woodwell also takes exception to Idso:

While Mr. Idso is correct that it is not possible to infer cause and effect from this record (of the Vostoc core data) and that the several reversals of the temperature trend are thought to have been caused by changes in the amount of solar energy received on earth, he has overlooked (the fact that) the single dominant pattern over 160,000 years was inconsistent with his hypothesis.

As temperatures and the concentration of carbon dioxide in the atmosphere rose in the past, there was no great surge in plant growth. Had there been the surge that he sees as so promising, the concentration of carbon dioxide in the atmosphere would not have continued to climb.[77]

Given these significant disagreements between a political leader and a scientific expert, and then the subsequent challenges to the position taken by Sherwood B. Idso, describe the process in which you would engage in order to determine which position was correct or more reasonable.

- How much scientific data would you need? What would you look up?

- Where would you go to find it?

• Would you want to consult with experts in the field of climate and agriculture? How would you go about identifying them?

• Do you think that expert opinion might be biased? What procedures would you employ to sift out the bias?

• Do you think that you will learn enough to be able to develop a hypothesis of your own? To whom would you turn in order to test out and debate your hypothesis?

• Would you be willing to present your hypothesis and supporting data to your classmates in the form of an oral or written report? Which form? Why or why not?

Questions for Discussion

1. What is being done in your community in regard to recycling solid waste, disposal of hazardous waste, and reduction of air and water pollution?

2. Is it correct to say that the earth is an endangered planet, or does such a statement exaggerate reality? Give at least four reasons in support of the position you take.

3. Discuss four reasons why it is a serious mistake to underestimate the soil and to take the soil for granted.

4. Describe the ecosystem of the tropical rain forest. Why are tropical forests cut down? What harmful consequences are caused by clearcutting tropical forests? In the long run, what advantages are obtained by eliminating tropical forests?

5. What connection exists between air pollution, acid rain, and the contamination of lakes in the northeastern United States? What measures need to be put in place to halt the pollution caused by acid rain?

6. What is meant by global warming or the greenhouse effect? If predictions about global warming come to pass, what will happen to agricultural areas and settlement patterns in the next century?

7. What function does ozone serve in the stratosphere? What harms to humans would result from increased ozone depletion? What steps can be taken to halt ozone depletion?

8. What ecological functions are served by oceans and fresh water bodies such as rivers and lakes? Name three kinds of pollutants which are capable of polluting either salt or freshwater. State two ways in which marine life can be harmed by pollution and two ways in which human life can be harmed.

For Further Reading

Lester R. Brown and Alan Durning, *State of the World* 1989 (New York: W. W. Norton & Company, 1989)

Will Steger and Jon Bowermaster, *Saving the Earth: A Citizen's Guide to Environmental Action* (New York: Alfred A. Knopf, 1990)

Scientific American, Special Issue: Managing Planet Earth, September, 1989, 261:3

Glossary

Alkaloids:	Organic substances containing nitrogen.
"Blue baby" syndrome:	A potentially fatal infant illness linked to nitrates in drinking water. Nitrates are an ingredient in fertilizer.
Catalyst:	A substance acting as an agent of change in a chemical reaction.
Crustacean:	Shellfish, including shrimp, crabs and lobsters.

Deforestation: To remove all or most of the trees of a forest, either to procure timber or to clear a space for development.

Depletion (of soil): To make infertile through overuse or unwise use.

Dioxin: A substance which has been linked to cancer in laboratory animals, it is one of the most toxic compounds known.

Ecosphere: The sum total of the interacting biological and physical factors on the planet earth.

Ecosystem: A unit of physical and biological elements that together form a system in which there are ordered or regulated flows of energy and apportionments of available nutrients.

Estuary: A body of water in which inflowing freshwater meets and mixes with saltwater.

Exponentially rising rate of depletion: An alarmingly high rate of loss according to which depletion in subsequent periods of time is much greater than double the original rate, going from OR^2 to OR^3 to OR^4 to OR^5, etc. (OR means Original Rate.)

Fallow: Land that has lain untilled and unseeded for a year or more in order to become richer.

Genetic diversity: The number of species that have been formally described (given a Latin name) is approximately 1.4 million. Estimates on the number of actual species in existence go as high as 30 million. Regardless of the exact number, the earth is habitat (home) to an extraordinarily diverse genetic population.

Groundwater: Water contained beneath the ground in aquifers; may be located at shallow or very considerable depths.

Habitat: The region where a plant or animal naturally lives.

Hectare: A unit of land measure; one hectare equals 2.47 acres.

Industrial Revolution: In the middle of the Nineteenth Century the United States and the nations of Western Europe turned from agriculture and home-based work to manufacturing, thus bringing about the Industrial Revolution.

Invertebrates: Animals which have no backbone.

Kilometer: A unit of length equal to 1,000 meters; 3,280.8 feet.

Nonbiodegradability: Substances, such as plastic, which do not break down over time when exposed to the elements and bacteria are said to be nonbiodegradable.

Organic matter: Derived from the living organisms which inhabit the earth such as plant life, worms, etc.

Organic way
(to build up nutrients
in soil):
Using vegetative matter and mulch to fertilize and restore the soil instead of chemical fertilizers.

Organization for Economic
Cooperation and
Development:
A voluntary association of 24 nations with headquarters in Washington, D.C. The nations are: Australia, Austria, Belgium, Canada, Denmark, Finland, France, Germany, Greece, Iceland, Ireland, Italy, Japan, Luxembourg, the Netherlands, New Zealand, Norway, Portugal, Spain, Sweden, Switzerland, Turkey, the United Kingdom and the United States.

Oxidant:
An oxidizing agent in a chemical reaction.

Polychlorinated Biphenyls
(PCBs):
Toxic chemicals, long used by industry, which are in the form of a thick, odorless liquid, and can be found on some river bottoms.

Radioactive Waste
or Nuclear Waste:
In low level form: compacted trash, contaminated clothing and hardware from nuclear plants, and sandy residues of mining and processing. In high level form: Fuel rods and waste left from fuel rods; these are found in nuclear power plants and plants which reprocess spent fuel.

Salinization:
The process by which the mineral content of a soil is increased, frequently as a result of poor irrigation techniques.

Scrubbers:

Devices found in smokestacks which run smoke through lime or limestone, removing approximately 95 percent of sulfur dioxide. The process usually employs water to bind the SO^2 chemically. The chemical waste which remains is toxic and presents a disposal problem.

Three Mile Island:

Site of a nuclear plant accident near Middletown, Pa. on March 28, 1979 in which a small quantity of radioactive gas was vented to the outside atmosphere.

Vinblastine:

The sulfate salt of an alkaloid extracted from *Vinca rosea.* Administered intravenously, it is used in the palliative treatment of lymphomas.

Vincristine:

The sulfate salt of an alkaloid extracted from *Vinca rosea.* Administered intravenously, it is used as an antineoplastic (an agent checking the maturation and development of malignant cells) especially in the treatment of acute leukemia.

Water Table:

The top of the zone of saturation in an aquifer.

End Notes

1. "Earth" and "Man, Prehistoric or Early Man" in *The New Columbia Encyclopedia* (New York: Columbia University Press, 1975), pp. 821, 1677.

2. Charles F. Bennett, *Conservation and Management of Natural Resources in the United States* (New York: John Wiley & Sons, 1983), P.31.

3. Paul Lewis, "World Population Will Top 6 Billion," *The New York Times*, May 15, 1990, p. A9.

4. Sandra Postel, "Halting Land Degredation," in Lester R. Brown, ed., *State of the World 1989* (New York: W. W. Norton & Company, 1989), p. 21.

5. ibid.

6. Pierre R. Crosson and Norman J. Rosenberg, "Strategies for Agriculture," *Scientific American*, September, 1989, 261:3, P. 131.

7. Bennett, p. 26.

8. Crosson and Rosenberg, p. 132.

9. Postel, pp. 26, 27.

10. "New Fears on Chemicals and Nervous System," *The New York Times*, May 17, 1990, p. A17.

11. Jodi L. Jacobson, "Abandoning Homelands," in *State of the World*, p. 67.

12. Anthony De Palma, "U. S. to Clean Radium Sites in Three Towns," *The New York Times*, June 7, 1990, pp. B1, B4.

13. Jacobson, p. 69.

14. Gerald E. Cavanagh and Arthur F. McGovern, "The Environment: Clean Air, Water, and the Corporation," in Cavanagh and McGovern, *Ethical Dilemmas in the Modern Corporation* (Englewood Cliffs, NJ: Prentice Hall, Inc., 1988), p. 147.

15. Robert D. Hamrin, *A Renewable Resource Economy*, (New York: Praeger, 1983), p. 26.

16. W. Jackson Davis, *The Seventh Year* (New York: W. W. Norton & Co., Inc., 1979), pp. 38-40.

17. Hamrin, p. 17.

18. Timothy Egan, "10,000 Are Expected to Lose Jobs to Spotted Owl," *The New York Times*, April 28, 1990, p. 8.

19. Edward O. Wilson, "Threats to Biodiversity," *Scientific American*, September, 1989, 261:3, p. 108.

20. Philip Shabecoff, "Loss of Tropical Forests Is Found Much Worse Than Was Thought," *The New York Times*, June 8, 1990, p. A1.

21. p. A1.

22. Wilson, p. 108.

23. p. 112.

24. Donald A. Falk, "What Kind of Stewards of the Planet Are We?" *The New York Times*, (Letters), June 5, 1990, p. 28.

25. pp. 114, 116.

26. p. 114.

27. Shabecoff, "Loss," p. B6.

28. p. A1.

29. Jill Schensul, "Each of Us Can Make a Difference," *The Record*, November 12, 1989, p. L1.

30. Hamrin, p. 24.

31. p. 25.

32. Will Steger and Jon Bowermaster, *Saving the Earth: A Citizen's Guide to Environmental Action* (New York: Knopf, 1990), p. 49.

33. United States Environmental Protection Agency, *The Public's Role in Environmental Enforcement*, Office of Enforcement (LE-133), March, 1990, p. 3.

34. Neil H. Reisner, "Poisons in Suburbia's Air," *The Record*, April 22, 1990, p. 3. The data presented are based on direct workplace exposure. Reisner states, "Information on the potential health impacts of community exposure is limited" but he says that some of these chemicals are released into the air to the detriment of people who live near the firms which use the chemicals.

35. Cynthia Pollock Shea, "Protecting the Ozone Layer," in *State of the World*, p. 84.

36. Steger and Bowermaster, p. 45.

37. Shea, p. 84.

38. Michael Renner, "Enhancing Global Security," in *State of the World*, p. 97.

39. p. 98.

40. p. 106.

41. p. 106.

42. Steger and Bowermaster, p. 107.

43. p. 74.

44. pp. 75, 76.

45. Hamrin, p. 43.

46. Steger and Bowermaster, p. 76.

47. p. 81.

48. Stephen H. Schneider, "The Changing Climate," in *Scientific American*, p. 74.

49. p. 75.

50. Steger and Bowermaster, p. 12.

51. Schneider, p. 77.

52. Lester R. Brown, Christopher Flavin and Sandra Postel, "A World at Risk," in *State of the World*, p. 11.

53. Schneider, p. 75.

54. p. 76.

55. Philip Shabecoff, "Scientists Predict Faster Ozone Loss," *The New York Times*, 6-24-90, p. 13, and Shea, p. 83.

56. p. 78.

57. p. 81. Shea quotes from National Aeronautics and Space Administration (NASA), "Executive Summary of the Ozone Trends Panel," Washington, D.C., March 15, 1988.

58. Thomas E. Graedel and Paul J. Crutzen, "The Changing Atmosphere," in *Scientific American*, p. 64.

59. Shea, p. 93.

60. Steger and Bowermaster, p. 169.

61. p. 168.

62. J. W. Maurits la Riviere, "Threats to the World's Water," in *Scientific American*, p. 89.

63. Steger and Bowermaster, p. 169.

64. p. 177.

65. la Riviere, p. 80.

66. p. 86.

67. Steger and Bowermaster, p. 192.

68. p. 201.

69. p. 201.

70. Postel, p. 42.

71. p. 50.

72. Bennett, 201.

73. Al Gore, Jr., "To Skeptics on Global Warming," *The New York Times*, April 22, 1990, p. 27.

74. Sherwood B. Idso, "Carbon Dioxide Warming Is Good for the Planet," (Letters), *The New York Times*, May 7, 1990, p. 14.

75. p. 14.

76. Raymond D. Clarke, "Don't Count on Carbon Dioxide to 'Enrich' the Earth," (Letters), *The New York Times*, May 24, 1990, p. 24.

77. George M. Woodwell, "What Plant Growth?" (Letters), *The New York Times*, May 24, 1990, p. 24.

Chapter Two

Making an Ethical Case for Environmental Responsibility

Introduction

The earth's soil, air and waters have been fouled by human actions. There are frightening warnings about what the future holds in store should climate changes continue unabated. Increasing depletion of the ozone layer which screens out the sun's ultraviolet rays is a disaster in the making. And the rate at which species—some of which have never even been identified—are becoming extinct is cause for alarm. Although some environmentally conscious individuals have long been aware of the harms attendant to ecological degradation, it is only relatively recently that widespread attention has been focused on environmental concerns and the way in which human actions can affect the environment. Indeed, some are suggesting that in the 90s we are going to change from the "me generation" to the "we generation" with a common focus on restoring the environment.

Awareness of the human dimension inevitably leads to the raising of ethical questions. These questions, in turn, give rise to the realization that when the subject is ethics and the environment there are few simple or self-evident answers. This chapter, therefore, will be concerned with what "traditional ethics" is and how human environmental responsibility might be understood within the context of traditional ethics. Alternate ethical approaches and their presuppositions will also be examined so as to determine how human environmental responsibility might be understood within these perspectives.

The Traditional Approach to Environmental Responsibility: Anthropocentrism

Ethics is a field of inquiry and reflection which is concerned with proper human conduct. Ethical inquiry examines the appropriateness of human action under all kinds of circumstances. The ethical task is largely analytical and the ethical position which is assumed rests on the contention that one response rather than another is morally appropriate based on rational justification or appeal to some other criterion.[1] There is general agreement about some ethical conclusions; e.g., that murder, rape and stealing are wrong. There is corresponding disagreement about other ethical conclusions, e.g., that it would always be wrong to use nuclear weapons in time of war, regardless of the circumstances.

In most traditional ethical analyses there are implicit presuppositions. One of the most pervasive is that human persons are alone among species in their ability to reason with their intellect and to exercise freedom in choosing to act or to abstain from acting. Knowledge and freedom imply responsibility and according to the traditional view, one aspect of responsibility is that humans should exercise appropriate concern about other forms of life. These other forms of life are considered to be less nobly endowed than the human species. It is argued that animals are ruled by instinct; in contrast to humans, they neither reason nor choose. Similarly, vegetative life follows the law which is inbred in it: trees, accordingly, always bring forth leaves in the spring and shed them in the autumn. It would be unthinkable for trees to do otherwise. Humans, on the other hand, can choose to sleep during daylight hours and to work at night; they have instincts, but they need not follow them. And while their growth and many of their characteristics are inbred, they are not preprogrammed in regard to where they will go, what they will do, or how they will treat one another.

They can choose to go on hunger strikes or to aid or ignore others who are in distress. Since humans are free they can exercise self-determination in both predictable and unpredictable ways.

When humans are set apart from the other mammalian species on the basis of characteristics peculiar to the human species, it is usually taken for granted that humans are superior to other life forms and are therefore entitled to a reasonable use of the land, the air, the waters, animals, fish and birds in order to meet their needs. Humans are therefore said to have a right to use the environment based on their superiority, along with a corresponding responsibility not to be cruel to sentient nonhuman beings and not to misuse or degrade nature. Within this perspective humans are thought to stand above all other species or to be properly situated at the center of the universe. Each and every nonhuman species is then evaluated in relation to its usefulness to humans. Accordingly, one purpose of animal flesh is to provide protein for the human diet, one purpose of beaches and wilderness is to provide recreational areas for humans, and a primary reason why birds chirp is to provide delight to the human spirit. An ethical mandate to preserve the environment so that it can continue to serve humans would be acknowledged. The wrongness of releasing harmful chemicals into the air would be readily admitted based on the knowledge that these chemicals cause injury to humans and other species which are useful to humans. Similarly, it would be considered immoral purposely to contaminate the marine food chain because people could get sick from eating contaminated fish. Within such an *anthropocentric* worldview, human needs and concerns are of central import and other species are understood as existing solely to serve human needs.

The Ten Commandments of Anthropocentric Environmentalism

The Ten Commandments of Anthropocentric Environmentalism might be formulated as follows.

1. You shall never underestimate the dignity which you possess because you are human and you can reason and choose.

2. You shall be responsible in your use of the goods of nature and you shall not take more than is reasonable.

3. You shall not intentionally pollute the soil, the air or the waters.

4. You shall become well informed so that you do not cause pollution through ignorant use of harmful substances or by accident.

5. You shall not be cruel to any sentient being or cause any living species to become extinct unless absolutely necessary.

6. You shall simplify your lifestyle and shall rely less on nonrenewable natural resources.

7. You shall recycle 50% or more of the solid waste you generate and shall avoid, as far as possible, using disposable products.

8. You shall plant trees to replace those which have been cut down so as to improve the quality of the air.

9. You shall become an advocate for species which lack the capacity to speak in behalf of their own well-being.

10. You shall resist the temptation to do nothing to repair the environment and shall instead join with others in your community and around the world to promote environmental responsibility.

Criteria Used to Evaluate Actions

It should be apparent that within traditional ethical systems humans consider themselves vested with the right to use the goods of nature and to determine what constitutes reasonable or unreasonable use. There are several ethical systems within the category "traditional ethics;" what they hold in common is the authority delegated to humans. However, the criteria by which a determination is made as to whether or not an action is ethically appropriate vary from one system to another. In *subjective approaches* to ethics individuals determine whether courses of action are right or wrong for them based on such factors as the way they feel, their intuitions, or the pleasure or pain they would experience in conjunction with the action. Subjective approaches offer few hard and fast value judgments because of the way in which they are attuned to the variable and unpredictable ways people feel and the ethical importance they attach to feelings per se. Thus, one person may find eating meat very pleasurable and consider it ethically acceptable, while another person may feel so repulsed by animal slaughter and the consumption of meat as to consider it ethically unacceptable.

Some ethical thinkers who see little likelihood of reaching a consensus on categorizing classes of actions as ethical or unethical propose a *utilitarian calculus* as the means for deciding which actions or courses of action should or should not be taken. Utilitarians hold that achieving the greatest good for the greatest number should be sought as an ethical goal. Given this contention, it follows that if there is an abundance of livestock worldwide, and if the meat provided by the livestock is a desirable source of protein, people should consume meat in order to gain necessary nutrients. But if there is a shortage of livestock worldwide and if these livestock consume a great deal of water and grain, thus causing worldwide food shortages, the eating of meat should be reduced and perhaps even eliminated so that an adequate supply of grain and water become available to the greatest number of people possible.

Advocates of the principle of universality argue that an action which is ethically appropriate for one person is ethically appropriate for any and all persons, and actions which are morally wrong for one person are morally wrong for any and all persons. A supporter of the norm that all acts of cruelty to animals are unethical, who equates slaughtering an animal with cruelty, and who adheres to the principle of universality, will contend that no animal should be slaughtered and, therefore, no person should eat meat.

The school of ethics known as natural law holds that persons should use their reason to act according to their human nature. Actions should be analyzed in order to determine whether or not they will promote a person's growth in humanity/integrity or retard such growth. Actions which would impede people from developing their goodness and virtue would be evaluated as unethical on *objective grounds*, while actions which would advance this goal would be assessed as ethical, likewise on objective grounds. Given the supremacy assigned to the human species by natural law proponents, as well as the functions assigned to intellect and will (the faculties which set humans above and apart), arguments based on animal rights would likely be rejected. Animals do not have rights; humans have rights to use animals. Arguments against cruel treatment of animals would be based on the fact that cruelty in any form debases humans and subjects animals to unnecessary pain. Arguments against eating meat based on the principle of distributive justice would, however, be given serious consideration. Distributive justice holds that each human person has a right to adequate nutrition so as to maintain dignity and wellbeing. If a clear and convincing case were made that the meat-eating people of the First World caused grain and water as well as meat to be scarce/unavailable to people in the Second and Third Worlds, then the natural law argument that affluent people should stop eating meat in order to enable nonaffluent people to obtain a share in the basics of a nutritional diet would probably be proposed.

The primary philosophical question relating to ethics and the environment concerns the adequacy and rationality of retaining anthropocentrism as the presupposed worldview. Those who challenge the anthropocentric approach argue that it would be ethically appropriate to replace the notion of human supremacy with some form of environmental egalitarianism within which non-human species are accorded rights or there are other fundamental changes in the ways humans understand their relationship to nonhuman species. In the following section we shall rely mainly on the developments outlined by Roderick Frazier Nash, Professor of History and Environmental Studies at the University of California at Santa Barbara, in his seminal work, *The Rights of Nature: A History of Environmental Ethics,* in order to note the major insights which have led to the challenge to anthropocentrism.

Alternate Approaches to Environmental Responsibility: A Non-Anthropocentric or Egalitarian Ethic

The idea that rights could be ascribed to nature represents a radical turn in human thought and has developed as a result of the promulgation of the insights of many influential environmentalists whose thinking can be categorized as non-anthropocentric or egalitarian. While it is important to become acquainted with the major environmentalists whose thinking gave rise to the notion of the rights of nature, it is also imperative to realize that, at the present time, the traditional anthropocentric perspective exists alongside, and has not been supplanted by, theories holding that life forms other than the human have rights.

Two men who lived in the United States during the nineteenth century exercised considerable influence on the way egalitarian environmental ethics would come to be framed by succeeding generations. Henry David Thoreau, author of *Walden Pond*, was a naturalist-philosopher who was virtually alone in 1857 in expressing such thoughts as his regard for "sunfish, plants, skunks, and even stars as fellows and neighbors . . . members of his community."[2] The woods through which Thoreau walked that year "were not tenantless, but choke full of honest spirits as good as myself any day."[3]

Similar egalitarian insight was expressed by John Muir who disappeared into the Canadian wilderness rather than answer the summons to serve in the Union Army during the Civil War. Profoundly affected by the time he spent in the wilderness, Muir's unique early insight was that nature existed for itself—apart from the usefulness it might hold for humans. In 1875 Muir wrote: "I have never yet happened upon a trace of evidence that seemed to show that any one animal was ever made for another as much as it was made for itself."[4] In later years John Muir retreated somewhat from his egalitarian position by proposing that national parks be established in wilderness areas to provide recreational space for human use.

Two early Twentieth Century proponents of thinking that nature was more nobly endowed than anthropocentrists held were

Albert Schweitzer and Aldo Leopold. Born in Alsace-Lorraine in 1875, and trained in philosophy, theology and music, Albert Schweitzer left a university professorship to study medicine; he subsequently practiced medicine as a missionary in Africa. Schweitzer's connection to the environmental movement stems from his articulation of a philosophy based on reverence for life. Writing in 1923, he established linkage between ethical human conduct and respect for the environment: The ethical person "shatters no ice crystal that sparkles in the sun, tears no leaf from its tree, breaks off no flower, and is careful not to crush any insect as he walks."[5] Schweitzer's ethic was not totally egalitarian, however, in that he approved of killing animals for medical research but only when "really and truly necessary" and when carried out with a compassionate sense of "responsibility for the life which is sacrificed."[6]

The last 25 pages of Aldo Leopold's *A Sand County Almanac*, published posthumously in 1949, contains his influential presentation of the basis for a land ethic. Leopold asserted a wholeness of life and matter and rejected a schema in which humans are the rulers of the universe: "We abuse land because we regard it as a commodity belonging to us. When we see land as a community to which we belong, we may begin to use it with love and respect."[7] His ideas have proven to be pivotal insights of egalitarian environmental ethics. Leopold argued that "a land-use decision is right when it tends to preserve the integrity, stability, and beauty of the *biotic community*. It is wrong when it tends otherwise."[8]

Beginning in the 1970s the thesis that moral rights do not begin and end with humans was appearing with increasing frequency in the writings of environmental advocates. In 1971 Harold Gilliam, an environmentalist and journalist, reported on a gathering held at the San Francisco Ecology Center. Its purpose was "to ask how the Bill of Rights might be rewritten . . . to affirm not only the rights of man but the rights of all living things—members of the Great Family." He went on to pose the memorable question: "What are the rights of a pelican? A redwood? A stream?"[9] The underlying purpose of the conference was to transform American government in order to include protection for the rights of nature within its constitutional tradition.

In a watershed article entitled "Should Trees Have Standing?" written in 1971, Christopher D. Stone proposed that society should "give legal rights to forests, oceans, rivers and other so-called 'natural objects' in the environment—indeed to the natural environment as a whole."[10] Stone held that just as humans could sue to collect damages for injuries received so, too, should creatures whose habitats were destroyed sue to receive payment to repair or replace their habitats. Stone said that human trustees or guardians should be appointed to collect fines and use the money for habitat restoration.[11] The fact that William O. Douglas, a Justice of the United States Supreme Court, used and approved of Stone's ethical position in a 1972 dissenting opinion added credibility to this surprising new way of thinking.

In 1976, John Lilly, an animal liberationist who agreed with Stone's thesis, extended its application to creatures of the sea. "Individual dolphins and whales are to be given the legal rights of human individuals. Human individuals and groups are to be given the right to sue on behalf of . . . *cetacean individuals* placed in jeopardy by other humans."[12]

In 1979, David E. Favre suggested that the United States Constitution be amended to include the statement that "all wildlife shall have the right to a natural life."[13] Realizing that in the absence of natural predation humans might need to check wildlife populations in the interests of the wildlife, Favre intended that the conferral of rights be on species and habitats rather than individual animals.[14]

Writing in 1973, Peter Singer linked the animal liberation movement to movements benefiting human minorities. He stated that animals should not be killed under any circumstances because animals feel pain. In view of this fact Singer argued for universal vegetarianism.[15] Like Peter Singer, Tom Regan, author of *The Case for Animal Rights* (1983), stated unequivocally that "the animal rights movement is a part of the human rights movement."[16] Regan contended that animals have a life and value of their own and rejected the notion that animals exist for humans.[17]

Holmes Rolston III, in *Environmental Ethics* published in 1988, stated that it is not humans who confer values on nature but rather nature which in itself is valuable. He said that the ordinary meaning of "Let the flowers live!" is "Leave the flowers for humans to enjoy." But he asked his readers to move beyond this ordinary meaning noting, "A thoroughgoing value theory in environmental ethics is more radical than this; it fully values the objective roots of value with or without their fruits in subjectivity."[18] Since values are antecedent to human valuers and not simply conferred by them, humans are seen by Rolston as having duties to animals, organisms, species and ecosystems. In contrast to environmentalists such as Gilliam, Stone, Lilly, Favre, Singer and Regan, who advocate rights for individual animals, species, vegetation, or the biosphere itself, Rolston preferred to formulate his ethical theory around the concepts of values and duties because of the inherent drawbacks he perceived in defining rights for nonhuman species:

> Humans do possess rights (that is, they can press claims on other humans about right behavior), and this use of "rights" may be contagious enough to work rhetorically with higher animals, whose claims can be pressed by sympathetic humans. But environmental ethics uses "rights" chiefly as a term of convenience; the real convictions here are about what is "right." The issues soon revert to what they always were, issues of right behavior by moral agents.[19]

J. Baird Callicott carried the notion of value to a radical conclusion when he reasoned that the life of a single organism of an endangered species is more valuable, more worthy of ethical respect by people, than the life of a person.[20] According to Nash, "From Callicott's ecocentric perspective even soil bacteria and oxygen generating oceanic plankton carried more ethical weight than beings at the tops of the food chains such as humans."[21] Environmentalists such as Rolston and Callicott are seen to represent a more inclusive and holistic approach to environmental ethics than advocates of animal rights such as Singer and Regan.

Deep Ecology and Ecofeminism

Deep ecology and ecofeminism are two branches of an egalitarian kind of environmental ethics. Each is distinguished by its own peculiar characteristics. Although there is no precise definition for the term "deep ecology," it is to this movement that Christopher and Judith Plant belong and of it that they write:

> Deep ecology is a significant strand of the *bioregional philosophy*. So termed by Norwegian philosopher, Arne Naess, to distinguish it from what he calls "shallow environmentalism" which works for minor reforms to the industrial system, deep ecologists seek major changes in the way those of us in dominant society view, and act in, the world. A primary shift required by the perspective of deep ecology is to a biocentric way of being: seeing all of life as sacred, not merely human beings, and acting upon that belief in all of our decisions.[22]

The history of deep ecology paralleled that of the presentation of arguments such as those just reviewed in favor of conferring rights on animals, trees, species and/or ecosystems. While not in conflict with the general thrust of the idea that nonhuman species should be thought of as possessing rights, deep ecology tends to incorporate much more than ethical arguments for rights within its philosophy. In a sense deep ecology is an alternate worldview with its own unique characteristics.

Deep ecology is very critical of the dominant strains in *Western Culture*, especially of the presumption that anthropocentrism is *normative*. As a consequence of their disapproval of anthropocentrism, deep ecologists tend to challenge the centrality traditionally given to the notions of conservation and stewardship. They reject the ideas that natural resources are contained within the earth for the use of humans and that humans act wisely and well when they put reasonable measures in place to conserve nature. They are also opposed to all human attempts to dominate or exploit nature. The wilderness is seen as existing for its own sake, not as a recreational space for humans or as the place to find species that might be useful to humans. According to deep ecologists there is no such thing as a pest; such entities as roaches and poison ivy should not be held in disesteem because they are troublesome to humans. Insects and weeds are part of the ecosystem and as such, deserve to be respected.

Deep ecologists assert that humans should try to become integrated into nature, fitting themselves to the land and living in harmony with it. Most deep ecologists are bioregionalists who believe that humans should find their work and sustenance in the region where they live rather than be dependent on motor vehicles to get to work and to transport their food. One of the most significant commitments bioregionalists make is to restore the damaged ecosystems which they discover in their region such as by bringing back species of fish which are native to local rivers and streams.

Deep ecology, in its various expressions, is not a monolithic approach to the environment. Numbered among deep ecologists are people who advocate holism. According to Aldo Leopold holism is the "indivisibility of the earth—its soil, mountains, rivers, forests, climate, plants, and animals," its wholeness as "a living being,"[23] so that humans are not considered distinct from other species. There are also deep ecologists who see each species as distinct but who emphasize that a core democracy exists in the biosphere, affording what might be termed "equal rights" to each individual species. The conferral of rights based on sentience would therefore be rejected because establishing sentience as a criterion is seen as creating a moral pecking order and setting some species above others. Regardless of whether deep ecologists advocate holism or a core democracy in the biosphere, they are united in their criticism of the harms anthropocentric humans have visited on the planet. For instance, deep ecologists argue that human population is growing beyond the ability of the earth to sustain human life. In their judgment, human over-consumption of the earth's resources as well as the destruction of natural habitats are among the most immoral of human deeds.

Some deep ecologists are willing to go so far as to take illegal actions in defense of nature. Dave Foreman of *Earth First!* provides his rationale for the *tree-spiking* and *monkey-wrenching* in which he has personally been involved:

I don't think monkey-wrenching is violence if you define violence as something against other life-forms. And I'm not sure that violence in and of itself is evil. Any creature will defend itself violently if pushed into a corner, and I don't think we overcome our problems by denying that basic animal instinct of self-preservation.

I think the whole concept of private property as a "good" has got to be replaced. There's a higher good out there than private property. A bulldozer is inherently a destructive agent. It can be used for good under certain circumstances, but its primary function is destruction. If they keep their bulldozers away from wild country, I'm not going to touch them. But when their bulldozer invades a wild place that I'm defending, then it's just self-defense. It's very easy not to have your machinery destroyed: just stay away from wild places![24]

Dave Foreman's identification with the place where he resides, his assignation of the right to be undisturbed to that "wild place," his argument that it can be morally right to render a bulldozer inoperable under certain circumstances, and his willingness to reject the validity of the theory of property rights represent an example of a radical expression of deep ecology.

During the past generation the feminist movement has exerted a significant influence in academic circles and in the broader culture as well. Like deep ecology, feminism is not a monolithic philosophy but is, rather, a way of thinking characterized by some specific insights. Among the commonly held feminist insights are that women are not inferior to men and that patriarchy (rule by the father or male rule) is not divinely ordained or normative according to a preestablished natural law which is somehow inherently knowable. Feminism argues against the status quo and for the equality of women and men in all spheres of life. It is totally opposed to blatant or subtle male dominance or exploitation of women. Ecofeminists contend that just as patriarchal males tend to depersonalize, objectivize and instrumentalize women (as sexual objects useful only for procreation, for example) and to treat women with disrespect by *using* them, so too, the earth tends to be understood as an object for exploitation within a patriarchal perspective.

In folklore and mythology the earth has been depicted as having a female identity. In a sense "Mother Earth" has been understood as giving life to and sustaining the life of all the inhabitants of the planet. People have always looked to the earth to exercise the feminine quality of nurturance: to provide the fruits which will sate their hunger, the shade which will enable their comfort, the sea breeze which will serve as the antidote for their stress. People have also been inclined to consider some aspects of nature as wild, uncontrolled and threatening. At their best the scientific and technological revolutions of the past century have enabled us to exercise mastery over nature for useful goals, but without much reflection on the ethical implications of interfering in the ecosphere. At their worst individuals, governments and corporations have raped virgin lands and fouled the air and waters while asserting the moral appropriateness of controlling or using nature which is intended to be the subject of human dominance.

In recent years feminist thinkers have registered outspoken opposition to the idea that it could be ethically right for humans to dominate nature. They have further disclosed the previously unspoken connection between the inclination to dominance or exploitation of women or the earth and a patriarchal worldview.[25] A feminist response to an anthropocentric and patriarchal approach to the earth suggests insights which would lead to a new way of understanding how humans should relate to the earth. Women naturally experience a feeling of kinship with the earth because both women and the earth bring forth life, and women understand how life-givers can come to be understood in an instrumental way as capable of fulfilling *only* a nurturing role. But it is the patriarchs who are likely to reach this conclusion and to exercise control and domination over creatures who are considered inherently inferior. Such an exercise denies the dignity of women and the integrity of the earth, while doing incalculable harm to both. Feminists, therefore, argue against giving approval to hierarchical structures which place men above women or humans above the earth. Instead they advocate an appreciation of the interrelatedness and symbiosis which in fact underlie the unity evident in the web of life. It is interesting to note the reasons feminists reject rights theory and language:

> According to (feminist) holistic or organic moral philosophy, it makes no more sense to assert the rights of, say, trees or animals against humans than it does to claim that the heart has rights in its relationship with the bloodstream or lungs. Ariel Kay Salleh has even asserted that most systems of morality that concern nature are weakened by a masculine preference for a hierarchy of rights of competing individuals. Ecofeminism, she asserts, is deeper than deep ecology.[26]

The Ten Commandments of Non-anthropocentric Environmentalism

As we have just seen, proponents of a non-anthropocentric perspective fall into several categories so that it is not possible to formulate directives upon which all would agree. In view of this fact I propose the Ten Commandments of Non-anthropocentric Environmentalism which follow. Numbers one through three would likely be accepted by proponents of animal rights, a *core democracy* in the ecosphere, holism, deep ecology and ecofeminism; in numbers four through ten I specify the particular group which would feel bound by each formulation.

1. You shall not pollute the land, the air or the waters, and shall not tolerate cruelty to any sentient beings.

2. You shall not, for any reason, destroy a habitat or ecosystem, or cause a species to become extinct.

3. You shall not content yourself with treating the symptoms of environmental degradation but shall labor tirelessly to correct the conditions and attitudes which give rise to environmental problems.

4. You shall not take the life of any animal for any reason except to free the animal from untreatable suffering. (Proponents of absolute animal rights)

5. You shall take the lives of animals only if the living conditions and slaughter of livestock are humane, or in order to carry out medical research which cannot be accomplished by any other means, or to prevent overpopulation, or to save your own life or that of another human who is threatened by an animal. (Proponents of limited animal rights)

6. You shall not esteem human life as higher than any other form of life and shall extend rights to all species, dismissing distinctions based on sentience. (Proponents of a core democracy in the ecosphere)

7. You shall understand yourself as related to all other species, coexisting with them in an intricate web of life, and shall make no distinctions between or among life forms which would imply human superiority. (Again, proponents of a core democracy)

8. You shall foster a sense of place, that is, identification with the region where you live, and you shall direct your efforts to renewing and restoring whatever damaged ecosystems you find there. (Proponents of deep ecology)

9. You shall reject all attempts to establish hierarchy including any arrangements which assign to humans power and dominion over nature. (Proponents of ecofeminism)

10. You shall not respect human laws, customs or procedures if these lead to pollution or the destruction of species or habitats, and you shall break the law when necessary to take action to prevent or reverse environmental degradation. (Proponents of the most radical deep ecology)

Underlying Issues to Be Resolved in Formulating a Coherent Ethical Response to the Environmental Crisis

Ethical judgments are statements about what should be done by humans. They proceed from an understanding of human nature and human personhood as well as an implicit *casuistry* about how intentions and circumstances impact the ethical status of actions. Given environmental consciousness, the whole field on which actions are played out, i.e., the environment, is fast becoming a constituent element to be considered in reaching ethical judgments.

Presuppositions concerning who the human person is, what the person's rights are vis-à-vis nature, what nature is and how nonhuman species ought to be understood as relating to the human need to be articulated and examined before human actions which affect the environment can be judged ethical or unethical. As we saw in the formulation of two sets of environmental commandments, the area of common ground is narrow: humans should not pollute the land, air and waters and they should not be cruel to sentient beings. According to Eric Katz, four issues need to be resolved before the area of agreement can be expanded:

> a. Instrumental vs. intrinsic value: Is nature valuable merely as it is used by humanity, or does it have value in itself?
>
> b. Anthropocentrism vs. non-anthropocentrism: Is an ethics of the environment based on human values, desires, and interest; or the values, desires and interests of nonhuman nature?
>
> c. Individualism vs. holism: Is our primary moral concern for individuals or for collections, groups, or systems?
>
> d. Shallow vs. Deep Ecology: Shallow ecology (also called "resource conservation") justifies environmental preservation on human interest grounds. Deep ecology calls for an expanded ecological consciousness which sees humanity unified with nature as a part of the system, not its ruler.[27]

The four issues which Katz identifies are profound and complex; they will not be quickly or easily resolved. It is important to be aware of the urgency of finding answers as well as the fact that these answers will lead to very specific harms or benefits to the environment. Certain attitudes will be necessary to promote the building of a consensus about human ethical responsibility to the environment. These include an openness to all ways of understanding nature with a corresponding willingness to admit and move beyond preconceived biases, and a willingness to compromise in order to achieve a goal which is mutually agreed upon. On the other hand, approaching a dialogue about environmental ethics with a closed mind, an opposition to making any revisions in one's attitudes or worldview, and an unwillingness to compromise will be counterproductive.

Reasons to Expect Humans to Act Responsibly Toward the Environment

There are four reasons to think that humans will turn from degrading the environment and will, instead, act responsibly. The first two reasons are based on capacities possessed by the human species alone: the possession of a conscience and the force of the aesthetic sense. The other two reasons are logical extensions of achievements humans already take pride in: the formulation of interhuman ethics and a track record in tackling systemic injustice.

Sane, mature humans attest to the experience of being accountable to conscience. Conscience is a *faculty* of the intellect which is capable of rendering judgments that particular actions or courses of action are morally right or wrong based on objective criteria. Through the deliberations of their consciences humans know that they should not pollute the air with asbestos particles because of the harmful health consequences to humans and potential damage to other living beings. Humans also know through the operation of conscience that advocacy and action on behalf of the environment are worthwhile pastimes. In saying that humans *know* this, I am not implying that the knowledge is comparable to that experienced in a feeling or a hunch. Rather, I mean that humans know that advocacy and action on behalf of the environment are good based on objective grounds. These could include the speculation that in the absence of explicit statements or actions nonaction or harmful actions would likely degrade the environment. A second basis could be rational agreement with positions presented by spokespersons for the environment who present convincing cases to justify their activism. The third and most compelling factor would probably be individual soul-searching to determine the components of an environmentally responsible deed, and personal conviction that the deed which is seen to be ethically appropriate and which seems to be mandated by the specific circumstances must be done.

The human experience of going through a process of discernment before arriving at a decision of conscience is complemented by a sense of serenity and integrity when the action chosen corresponds to the light of reason. On the other hand, a sense of guilt and remorse is experienced when humans go against their consciences. During our lifetimes, to the extent that we mature and develop as sensitive people, we come unmistakably to the realization that an overall sense of well-being is inextricably connected to adhering to the voice of conscience.

It is probably accurate to say that up until the publication in 1962 of Rachel Carson's *Silent Spring* and the celebration of the first Earth Day in 1970 there was widespread ignorance about environmental degradation. There may also have been a naive over-assessment of the earth's recuperative powers. In recent years, however, the publication of a plethora of books along with multi-faceted efforts by the media, classroom instruction and people's own experiences have made the ways the earth is endangered common knowledge. Human greed in exploiting the earth and shortsightedness in not taking ecological consequences into consideration have come to be evaluated as morally wrong. Coverage of such threats as global warming and ozone depletion has led people to argue that the safer course should now be followed because if we wait for unanimity from scientific experts it may be too late to halt/reverse atmospheric destruction. In essence what has happened is that humans have had their collective consciousness raised about the serious threats which endanger the planet and they are now using their new knowledge to reach decisions of conscience which are environmentally aware. De facto, human conscience has begun to admit responsibility for a sphere beyond the exclusively human and to exercise concern for the whole web of life.

Humans are unique in that they possess an aesthetic sense. Humans appreciate the wonder and beauty of the universe and they feel troubled when things of beauty are destroyed or the functioning of ecosystems is disrupted. It is the human aesthetic sense which reacts in outrage when medical waste washes up on a beach, when species are made extinct by the destruction of their habitats, or when animals are treated cruelly. The human aesthetic sense contains a strong moral component in that those human actions which attack the earth's beauty and order are apprehended as ethically wrong. The awareness that they should not be done arises spontaneously.

It goes without saying that humans need eyes in order to see and that the aesthetic sense does not function in the absence of perception. One effect of the recent development of environmental education has been to heighten our awareness of the interconnectedness of the millions of species within the web of life as well as the global nature of ecological interrelatedness. The fragile and intricate threads which connect species within the food chain, for example, are now apt to be recognized and the human aesthetic sense cannot help but respond decisively against the harms caused to many species by PCBs and DDT.

In our overview of non-anthropocentric approaches to environmental ethics we considered some reasons why human exercise of superiority over other species should not be justified. While harmful actions which issue from a sense of dominance are certainly wrong, it might make sense to appeal to the uniquely human characteristics of conscience and the aesthetic sense as two cornerstones of environmental ethics. In so doing an appeal would be made to the noblest qualities humans possess. Since the future of the planet depends upon a decision made by humans that the earth ought to be preserved, such a base may be the most realistic starting point.

The history of humankind is distinguished by the civilized arrangements into which people have entered. The basic rights to be let alone to pursue one's own goals and not to be injured have led to the setting of appropriate limits. A fundamental role of government is to protect individual rights and to punish or restrict persons who harm or threaten others. It is the human abilities to dialogue, to compromise and to create governing structures that have resulted in the formulation of agreed-upon norms of conduct and provision for oversight. By extension, I think that a common ground can be attained in respect to environmental ethics. While it is unrealistic to expect everyone to agree that trees should have legal standing and that nonhuman species possess a specific kind of worth (either intrinsic or instrumental), it is still possible to conceptualize and implement an ethics of environmental responsibility in a society that is ecologically aware and committed to the future of the earth. Anthropocentrists who argue for reasonable use of the environment will be forced to bear the burden of proof that a given intervention in an ecosystem is indeed reasonable and does not present a mortal threat to that system. If some anthropocentrists are incapable of convincing others of their contentions, I do not think that responding with violence against machinery or humans (as some radical deep ecologists advocate) is an appropriate answer. The reason I hold this opinion is because I place hope in the human ability to dialogue, negotiate and compromise because I think that trying to circumvent this process will undermine the hope for progress toward resolution, since neither side can expect to have all its demands met by forcing its case.

The final reason for expecting humans to put in place a plan for responsible treatment of the environment is that in recent history the realm of the ethical has been enlarged to include systemic inequities. While ethics is usually cast in individualistic terms, attention is gradually shifting to social problems confronting humankind. In this vein one readily thinks of concern about a militaristic spirit along with weapons of mass destruction, economic injustice, sexism and racism. People who understand how women and men have suffered as a result of the patriarchal bias ingrained in Western Civilization are very capable of carrying this insight over to an awareness of how arrogance has led to the exploitation of the earth. There is also likely to be a recognition that just as everyone suffers as a result of sexism, so the entire community of the biosphere suffers from clear-cutting Third World rain forests, incinerating fossil fuels in the Second World and releasing ozone-destroying substances in the First World. In a world that has become a global village, everyday it becomes easier to identify connections and to establish connectedness. I am convinced that this insight can facilitate the development of a comprehensive ethical response to the environmental crisis.

Conclusion

An ethical case for environmental responsibility can be made on the traditional grounds that humans should not harm the earth so that an undamaged planet will continue to sustain human life. Or the way humans relate to the planet can be examined in a more radical way with the intention of calling into question the assumption of human superiority, and condemning greedy, exploitative and ignorant humans for the harms they have visited on the earth. Whichever approach is adopted, there is a crucial urgency to act to halt environmental degradation and restore damaged ecosystems. Perhaps a promising path to this end consists in challenging humans to live up to their potential by being persons of conscience and by cultivating and attending to their aesthetic sense. Dialogue and compromise should be encouraged in order to attain a negotiated environmental ethics which is more interested in the integrity of the earth than the starting points from which the ethical system proceeds.

Case Study

On May 6, 1990, Molly O'Neill wrote the following in *The New York Times*:

> For generations, dairy has been synonomous with "pure," beef with "strong." And cattle have ranged over the soul of America, a symbol of wide-open spaces, broncobuster spirit and the bucolic life on the family farm.

> Then the all-American icon stumbled into a land-mined pasture. Environmentalists, politicians and consumers are debating whether the planet can sustain its cattle herd as the human population swells.

> In America, the cow is on trial. The charges include dietary wrongdoing, pollution and misuse of natural resources.

> There are compelling arguments on both sides of the cow case.

> Lean beef provides protein and iron; low-fat dairy products provide calcium and zinc. Cattle help maintain open space

and can feed on plants and grains that are unfit for human consumption.

Whose Grain?

On the other hand, there are health risks in a diet that is high in beef and dairy, and questions about the growth enhancers and antibiotics administered to cattle. And the amount of grain used to feed cattle in this country could help ease world hunger.

Cattle are linked with the erosion of topsoil and the agricultural runoff that damages streams. Worse yet, bovine flatulence generates a significant amount of methane, a greenhouse gas.

Recently, Elsie and Bossy have been called "public enemy No.1" and "nature's nuclear reactor."

Pound for pound, livestock outweighs humans four to one in the United States. Americans consume 106 grams of protein a day, said Dr. David Pimentel, professor of Agricultural Science at Cornell University. The recommended daily allowance is 54 grams of protein, he said; "we are eating way too much protein as a nation."

America's taste for cows had less environmental effect when the country was less densely settled. But today beef and dairy farming add to pollution, and concerns about national diet extend beyond personal health to the well-being of the planet.

In a 1988 report, the Environmental Protection Agency said agricultural runoff is "by far the most extensive source of pollution."

The agency is unable to determine what share of the problem is due to cattle, as opposed to fertilizers or pesticides. But Dr. Pimentel points out that livestock occupies almost half the land devoted to farming in the nation. The cattle runoff adds nitrogen to water, and the nitrogen promotes plant life, which can clog streams.

In The Feed Lots

Cattle growers don't disagree, at least when animals are crowded into feed lots. "When you pack cattle into feed lots they are going to be producing more manure than the lot can handle and you're going to get some runoff," said Bert Hawkins, president of Agri-Business, a consulting firm in Lake Oswego, Ore.

The industry has shortened the time that animals remain in feed lots. But for some environmentalists, this isn't enough. "Get rid of the confinement feed lot altogether," said Wes Jackson, founder of the Land Institute in Salina, Kan. "You don't have these problems when cattle graze the grasslands where they evolved and where they are part of a natural, balanced system."

For other environmentalists, that isn't enough, either. "This is just an interim remedy to the environmental disaster we have created through our food growing practices," said John Robbins, author of "Diet for a New America" (Stillpoint Publishing, 1987). "The only real solution is to find alternative food sources."

Kendal Frazier of the National Cattlemen's Association in Englewood, Colo., replied, "This is another example of taking a very important issue, our environment, and using it to promote a strictly vegetarian agenda."[28]

• Evaluate the arguments for and against continued reliance on cattle as a food source, and determine which approach is more convincing to you. State the reasons for your position.

• Identify any hints of anthropocentrism or non-anthropocentrism which you detect in positions for and against cows.

• Should cows continue to play a central role as providers of human dietary needs? Why or why not? If you have difficulty arriving at a definite answer to this question, what factors are holding you back?

• By means of what process ought this issue be resolved in the United States today? Are there any inherent weaknesses in the process which you advocate?

Questions for Discussion:

1. Do you think that it is possible to construct an irrefutable argument either for or against an anthropocentric view of nature? Why or why not?

2. If a person calls herself a conservationist and says that bias did not affect her in any way as she came to her position, what questions would you pose in order to suggest that she might actually hold biases?

If a person calls himself a proponent of a core equality in the ecosphere and argues that a roach has as much intrinsic worth as a person, and he says that he was not affected by bias in coming to his position, what questions would you pose in order to suggest that he might actually hold biases?

3. Henry David Thoreau said that "sunfish, plants, skunks, and even stars" were "members of his community." Who are the members of your community and what criteria do you use for establishing membership?

4. Do you think that it makes sense to extend moral rights to animals, various forms of vegetation or other nonhuman species and to designate humans to act as their trustees? Or do you think that it makes more sense to stress, as Holmes Rolston did, in what right human behavior toward the environment should consist? Support the position you favor by formulating three reasons to back it up.

5. Deep ecologists say that humans should walk lightly on the earth. Write a paragraph or outline a short oral presentation describing what "Walk lightly on the earth" means to you.

6. Tree-spiking and monkey-wrenching are two strategies suggested by radical proponents of deep ecology to keep natural ecosystems intact. Discuss the reasons why you agree or disagree with these strategies.

7. According to ecofeminists why has the naming of the planet "Mother Earth" led to its degradation? State why you agree or disagree with the analysis of ecofeminists.

8. In view of the profound differences between holders of anthropocentric and non-anthropocentric worldviews, to what common ground might we turn in order to begin to articulate and implement an ethics of environmental responsibility?

Debate

Resolved: That there is a core equality among all species in the ecosphere and that human customs, laws and ways of thinking should reflect this equality.

For Further Reading

Roderick Frazier Nash, *The Rights of Nature: A History of Environmental Ethics* (Madison, Wisc.: The University of Wisconsin Press, 1989).

Holmes Rolston, III, *Environmental Ethics: Duties to and Values in the Natural World* (Philadelphia: Temple University Press, 1987).

The journal *Environmental Ethics* which began publishing in 1979 is an excellent source for scholarly articles addressing the human relationship to the environment.

Glossary

Anthropocentric: Centering one's view of everything around the way it relates to the human species.

Bioregional Philosophy: Held by people who cultivate a love for and identification with a particular place as well as a resolve to live there in harmony with nature.

Biotic community: The particular ecosystem in which humans reside along with innumerable other species.

Casuistry: Subtle, intricate reasoning process about moral issues.

Cetacean individuals: Water mammals such as whales and dolphins.

Core democracy: An outlook which calls for a radical bioegalitarianism, that is, the equality of all species and equal "rights" of all.

Egalitarianism: Advocacy of full and complete equality for all persons; when carried over into an inclusive environmental ethics, the equality is extended to all species.

Faculty: A natural, specialized power of humans, such as the capacity to exercise rational judgment or to freely choose.

Monkey-wrenching: Rendering machinery inoperable by removing, disconnecting or destroying internal mechanisms.

Normative: Established as a standard or rule specifying what is to be done.

Objective grounds: Reaching decisions based on rational arguments which are characterized as logically convincing rather than on a subjective factor such as feelings which vary from person to person.

Subjective approaches: (to ethics) Reaching ethical judgments without recourse to objective and generally agreed upon standards.

Tree-spiking: Inserting metal spikes into trees in order to keep power saws from cutting through. Those who spike trees usually deliver anonymous warnings to logging companies so that logging operations can be canceled. If a logger's saw were to hit a spike, he/she would run the risk of serious injury from the deflected saw.

Utilitarian calculus:

Equating what is ethically correct with a measurement of what would bring about the greatest good for the greatest number.

Western Culture:

The skills and art (or the civilization) of people living in the Western hemisphere which have their roots in ancient Greece and Rome, Judeo-Christian beliefs and values, and the cumulative heritage of Europe and the Americas.

End Notes

1. For a concise and very readable summary of the various ways of approaching anthropocentric ethics, and especially helpful critiques of the criteria on which moral judgments are based, cf., Andrew C. Varga, *On Being Human*, (New York: Paulist Press, 1977).

2. Roderick Frazier Nash, *The Rights of Nature: A History of Environmental Ethics* (Madison, Wisconsin: The University of Wisconsin Press, 1989), p. 37.

3. Henry David Thoreau, *The Maine Woods*, Joseph J. Moldenhauer, ed., (Princeton, N.J., 1972), p. 181, as cited in Nash, p. 37.

4. *John Muir, A Thousand-Mile Walk to the Gulf*, William F. Bade, ed., (Boston, 1917), p. 343, as cited in Nash, p. 40.

5. Albert Schweitzer, *Philosophy of Civilization and Ethics*, John Naish, trans. (London, 1923), p. 254, as cited in Nash, p. 61.

6. Albert Schweitzer, *Out of My Life and Thought: An Autobiography*, (New York: 1933), p. 271, as cited in Nash, p. 61.

7. Aldo Leopold, *A Sand County Almanac* (New York, 1949), pp. 203-4, as cited in Nash, p. 69.

8. Leopold, pp. 224-225, as cited in Nash, p. 71.

9. p. 128.

10. Christopher D. Stone, "Should Trees Have Standing? Toward Legal Rights for Natural Objects," (Los Altos, Calif., 1974), p. 9, as cited in Nash, p. 128.

11. p. 129.

12. John Lilly, "The Rights of Cetaceans under Human Laws," *Oceans 9*, March, 1976, pp. 67-68, as cited in Nash, p. 132.

13. Nash, p. 132.

14. p. 132.

15. p. 138.

16. Tom Regan, *The Case for Animal Rights* (Berkeley, Cal., 1983), p. xiii, as cited in Nash, p. 143.

17. p. 143.

18. Holmes Rolston, III, *Environmental Ethics: Duties to and Values in the Natural World* (Philadelphia: Temple University Press, 1988), p. 116.

19. p. 51.

20. Nash, p. 153.

21. p. 153.

22. Christopher Plant and Judith Plant, *Turtle Talk: Voices for a Sustainable Future* (Philadelphia: New Society Publishers, 1990), p. 68.

23. Aldo Leopold, in Eugene C. Hargrove, "Some Fundamentals of Conservation in the Southwest," *Environmental Ethics 1*, Summer, 1979, pp. 139-140, as cited in Nash, p. 66.

24. An interview with Dave Foreman, "Becoming the Forest In Defence of Itself," in Plant, p. 63.

25. Several references to writers on the connection between patriarchy and the exploitation of the earth are suggested in Nash, p. 253.

26. p. 146. The citation to Ariel Kay Salleh's work which is mentioned in the quote is: "Deeper than Deep Ecology: The Eco-Feminist Connection," *Environmental Ethics*, Winter, 1984, 339-345.

27. Eric Katz, "Environmental Ethics: A Select Annotated Bibliography, 1983-1987," *Research in Philosophy & Technology*, 9, 1989, p. 253.

28. Molly O'Neill, "Cows in Trouble: An Icon of the Good Life Ends up On a Crowded Planet's Hit Lists," *The New York Times*, May 6, 1990, p. E1.

Chapter Three

The Role of Religious Insight in the Formulation of a Response to the Environmental Crisis

Introduction

Many human questions are deep and perplexing, having to do with the fundamental meaning and purpose of life. Answers to these so-called "ultimate questions" inevitably include a religious component. The action, permission, will or design of God is almost always implicated in response to such queries as: Who am I? What am I supposed to do during my lifetime? Why are humans sometimes kind and cruel at other times? What is the meaning of love? Why do bad things happen to good people? What will happen to me when I die? Another ultimate question concerns how the universe came to be and why the earth took on characteristics which make it habitable for humans. People of faith believe that the earth's origin is attributable to the creative act of God. It is within the context of their religious traditions that they seek to discover why humans have become the affliction of the earth and how religious insight might lead to an ethic of environmental responsibility.

What people believe about who God is exerts a strong influence on their attitudes and actions. If belief is in a *transcendent* God, conceived as a strict and demanding judge, then people will tend to approach this God in a fearful, guarded way. When God's *non-corporeality* and other-worldliness are emphasized along with transcendence, believers may be apt to think of God as disengaged from the earth and its processes. On the other hand, when God is understood as *immanent* and approached as a loving Mother and Father who is intimately involved with creation, then people will tend to feel a comfortable trust in a deity who is related to them. Just as a writer becomes present to her readers through her prose or poetry, and an artist through the canvas, so an immanent God becomes manifest through the works of creation. It goes without saying that within such a scenario these works call forth esteem, not indifference. (Please note that the transcendence of God is misunderstood when it is conceived in opposition to God's immance so that God is thought of as transcendent *or* immanent, with believers choosing to relate to one or the other God. In addition, one should not think of the transcendent God as a strict judge to be feared; rather, one should approach God mindful of the mighty, awesome powers which are rightly attributed to God.)

As we shall see in this chapter, the inclination to become engaged or disengaged in nature is frequently derived from one's *concept of God.* A direct connection is generally apprehended between one's beliefs about what God wills and the way humans treat the earth. A religiously-based defense of anthropocentrism is generally tied to the belief that God entrusted humans with stewardship, dominion or control over the earth. Thinking of the earth as one half of the pair "earth and heaven" frequently results in an unfavorable comparison of earth to heaven with the assignation of less value to earth than to heaven. Believing that the earth will eventually "pass away" while heaven will endure eternally can lead to a disinterest in or dismissal of the things of earth, including environmental concerns. Believing that God's greatness is manifest in her creation, however, leads to a deep and wondrous appreciation of it. When this belief is coupled with a sense of human relatedness to all God's other creatures, the earth is approached with reverence and environmental concerns are taken to heart.

Religious doctrines, that is, what religions teach about such subjects as who God is and how God intends that humans should conduct themselves on earth, as well as church-formulated moral norms for human action have traditionally provided guidance for believers. In general, *Eastern religions, pre-patriarchal religions* and *Native American religions* have tended to understand gods or God as present to or active in creation. Within the main strands of the *Judeo-Christian tradition*, however, God has tended to be understood as above and apart from creation. It might be more correct to say that the issue of how God interacts with nature has, for the most part, been unexamined because, until rather recently, it has not occurred to *theologians* or other members of religious communities to raise it. Given the pressing nature of contemporary environmental problems, and the critical issue of how God wants humans to treat the earth, there is no doubt that the time is at hand for a thorough exploration of this matter.

As far as a Judeo-Christian formulation of environmental ethics is concerned, a comprehensive body of doctrine has not been formulated. In fact, to date little attention has been paid to concern for the earth. Philosophical critiques of anthropocentrism have largely gone unanswered or have been addressed in a superficial manner. There is no question that it is a matter of urgent importance for church leaders together with the "sane, rational, dreamless people" (to use Thomas Berry's characterization) who sit in the pews to explore the links between religious faith and environmental ethics in order to participate in the process of healing the earth.

Is there a Connection between the Judeo-Christian Tradition and the Environmental Crisis?

Some people contend that beliefs embodied in the Judeo-Christian tradition have contributed to human attitudes and actions which have resulted in the degradation of the earth. Others counter that the norms, values and wisdom inherent in the Judeo-Christian tradition have the potential of leading to the solution of the environmental crisis. Which one of these propositions is true, or closer to the truth? Let us consider in turn the argumentation on which each is based in order to be prepared to make an assessment.

An Examination of the Thesis that Religiously-Derived Anthropocentric Attitudes Have Motivated the Western Assault on Nature

In March, 1967 Lynn White wrote a provocative article entitled "The Historical Roots of Our Ecological Crisis" which appeared in *Science* magazine. White's thesis was presented within the short span of five pages; his contention was that the Judeo-Christian tradition preached the message that it is wrong to exploit people but it is right and proper to exploit nature. He argued that an irreverent or dismissive attitude towards nature is grounded in Christian dogma and is widely accepted in the Western Hemisphere among both Christians and non-christians. White pointed out that the belief that God planned all of creation for the benefit of the human prevented humans from acknowledging that nature had any value in itself. By destroying pagan animism, he contended, Christianity made it possible to exploit nature in a mood of indifference to natural objects. According to White, the ecological crisis would not be resolved through the application of scientific or technological remedies; he saw the roots of humankind's trouble as largely religious, requiring a rethinking of the relationship between God, humans and the rest of creation as the first and most important step to be taken.[1]

White concluded that Christianity was the most anthropocentric religion that the world had seen and that the environment had suffered incalculably as a result of rationalizations derived from anthropocentrism.

Five factors in addition to anthropocentric interpretations of biblical stewardship texts have been cited as giving rise to an irreverent attitude towards nature. Let us consider each in turn.

First. The Judeo-Christian tradition began with the rejection of pantheism and the adoption of radical monotheism. Pantheistic religions, also known as pagan religions, were distinguished by the practice of worshiping many gods. Usually these gods were associated with nature; e.g., Poseidon, the Greek god of the sea and Gaia, the Greek earth goddess. Identifying gods with natural objects or processes sacralized nature, insuring its special status. The Hebrew people, in adopting a radical monotheistic faith, rejected pagan belief in many gods. Hebrew faith was directed to Yahweh, one God, almighty and transcendent who stood above and apart from nature. Yahweh created nature and was not frightened or threatened by thunder or flood. In becoming radical monotheists, the Hebrews and their Christian descendants refused to identify God with nature and articulated a belief in God's power over nature. By separating God from nature the earth may have become less holy to monotheists than it had been to pantheists.

Second. One characteristic which set the early Christians apart was their *eschatology.* The first few generations of Christians were close in time to the historical Jesus and it was their deeply held belief that Jesus' second coming was imminent. In Christian belief the second coming will usher in the final phase of human history after which earth and time will end and God's eternal kingdom will be fully realized. The first generations of Christians, imbued as they were by a sense of anticipation for what they believed would soon come about, are generally depicted as exhibiting little interest in the things of earth. Even though the eagerly awaited second coming of Christ, with the concomitant end of time, did not come to pass in their lifetimes, the tendency of the early Christians not to attach much value to the things of earth became part of the legacy they passed on to succeeding generations.

Third. Dualism is an approach to thinking which divides something into two parts; *duo* is Latin for two. When the subject under consideration is reality, that is, all that is, and the assumption is that reality consists in such components as earth and heaven, time and eternity, matter and spirit, evil and good, nonhuman beings and human beings, dualists disvalue the first member of each pair and value the second. Dualism traces its roots to Greek philosophy and was given voice in early Christianity by Greek and Jewish converts who were influenced by Greek culture. As with the eschatological attitude that devalued the earth, so, too, a dualistic outlook has become entrenched within Christianity to the detriment of the earth.

Fourth. Asceticism, a practice associated with some Hebrew religious communities, has been embraced by Christians throughout the centuries. Asceticism requires self-denial and discipline of the body so as to enable one to reject sin and draw close to the all-holy and transcendent God. One feature of asceticism is the wariness it cultivates toward the body. The human body is considered separate from and of lesser value than the human soul or spirit. The body is held in suspicion because its demands occupy a person's time and attention and are an obstacle to the soul's communion with God. In addition, the body's pursuit of pleasure through such activities as eating, drinking and sex are viewed negatively. If intemperate, these activities are sinful and, if temperate, they are assessed as less beneficial to humans than such activities of the spirit as prayer and contemplation. Their thinking that matters of the spirit are more worthy of human interest and devotion than concerns of the flesh prompt ascetics to dismiss the earth and the things of nature as unimportant.

Fifth. Both the Hebrew and Christian faiths have been organized along patriarchal lines. Patriarchy is a system of social organization in which the head of a tribe or a family is male, descent is traced through the male line and the eldest son inherits headship and ownership of family property when the father dies. In patriarchal religions the rabbi, priest or minister is male and maleness is attributed to God. Male metaphors for God such as Father, King, Ruler and Lord are commonly used, as are male pronouns. Patriarchal systems, religious and secular, are arranged along hierarchical lines. Ranks or grades are established with the higher ranking males having authority over those lower in rank, and the male highest in command having authority over all. Traditionally a male deity has been conceptualized as sitting atop the structure and validating the entire arrangement. Anthropocentrism is the logical corollary of patriarchal-hierarchical religious systems. The superior status of the male human is taken for granted along with the assumption that the goods of nature, ranked far below humans in the grading system, exist solely for the use of humans.

One aspect of patriarchal-hierarchical systems is the second class status relegated to women. This relegation is justified by asserting that women are inherently inferior to men. They are thought to be irrational, weak and incapable of fulfilling demanding intellectual, leadership or priestly roles. The kind of roles women are considered fit to exercise are either servile in nature or directly linked to the female biological capacity for motherhood. God is credited with designing females for such tasks.

Within patriarchal religious traditions there is also a tendency to view females with suspicion—as temptresses whose wiles threaten male purity and virtue. A carryover to nature which has traditionally been represented by female metaphor is suggested in a dominating attitude toward the earth which requires that men tame and subdue it. There may also be a carryover in the ideology of the industrial and technological revolutions that it is proper for nature to submit to the control of powerful males.

In summation, in Genesis God is depicted as giving human beings "dominion over the fish in the sea, the birds of the air, the cattle, all wild animals on land, and everything that creeps on earth." (Gen. 1:26) It was up to humans to interpret what "dominion" meant and how "dominion" should be exercised. In view of the fact that religious beliefs were skewed by a negative or indifferent attitude toward the earth as well as an inflated assessment of the status delegated to men by God, it is not surprising that abuse and exploitation of the earth were rationalized as permissible exercises of dominion.

The issue of whether or not the adoption of monotheism, along with an eschatological outlook focused on the end time, pervasive dualistic, ascetic and patriarchal-hierarchical influences originating in the Judeo-Christian tradition have been exercised to the detriment of the earth is a crucial one. In order to address it fairly, let us consider how an alternative assessment of these and other significant aspects of this tradition might actually provide the rationale for respecting and healing the earth.

An Examination of the Thesis that the Judeo-Christian Tradition Provides Motivation for an Attitude of Caring toward the Earth

The thesis that the Judeo-Christian tradition contains insight which will motivate people to adopt an attitude of caring toward the earth is supported by six arguments.

First. Lynn White's critique of Western religion is assessed as containing grains of truth but, overall, it is evaluated as simplistic and unconvincing.[2]   Scholarly analysis of what the *author of Genesis 1:26* had in mind when he related how God had given the human species dominion over the rest of creation does not include any right to abuse or exploit nature. Genesis 1:26, along with Genesis 3:23 which records how God entrusted to Adam (humankind) the work of tilling the earth, are interpreted as requiring humans to manage the land in a caring way so as to sustain themselves and to be able to pass an intact ecosphere on to their children. If human arrogance distorts the biblical notion of dominion and undermines the respect inherent in the attitude with which people are supposed to approach the land, then human sinfulness should be blamed, not the scripture texts. The concept of stewardship which implies the human responsibility to exercise prudence and care in tending the land is certainly anthropocentric, but the anthropocentrism is nuanced so as not to allow crassness toward nature or disdain for any being. Just as the Israelite kings understood the authority which they exercised as requiring care for their subjects, especially the poor and the weak, along with concern for their well being and prosperity, it follows that humans should seek to nurture a similar attitude toward the earth.

Second. The Judeo-Christian tradition which is radically monotheistic incorporates both panentheism and the notion of God's immanence into its doctrine. Panentheism means that God is in everything and everything is in God. The stamp of God's hand is seen in nature because each and every species is truly God's handiwork. In another sense, God is perceived to be the ground of all being and every living thing has the source of its life in God. A panentheistic faith permits the erection of no barriers between God and God's creation because it does not make sense to separate the millions of species which are in existence from God who created and sustains them.

The lyrics of two popular religious hymns convey a panentheistic sense:

> O Lord my God, when I in awesome wonder
> Consider all the works thy hands hath made,
> I see the stars, I hear the rolling thunder,
> Thy pow'r throughout the universe displayed;
> Then sings my soul, my Savior God, to thee,
> How great thou art! How great thou art!
> ("How Great Thou Art")

and:

> Field and forest, vale and mountain,
> flowery meadow, flashing sea,
> Chanting bird, and flowing fountain
> call us to rejoice in thee.
> ("Joyful, Joyful We Adore Thee")

The belief that God is immanent means that God is present to humans, with them and within them. People pray to God who is in their heart; when the road of life is toughest, according to the popular poem *Footprints*, the Lord is depicted as carrying vulnerable suffering persons on his shoulders. "My precious, precious child, I love you and I would never leave you. During your times of trial and suffering, when you see only one set of footprints (in the sand), it was then that I carried you."

Third. Although the eschatological view that the end of time is near can be viewed as leading to a disparaging attitude toward the earthly realm, a far more important Christian belief, that in the goodness of all life created by God overshadows the negativism toward nature which may be generated by Christian eschatology. We read in Genesis that "God saw all that God had made, and it was very good." (Gen. 1:31) That the goodness of nature should be proclaimed so unequivocally and reaffirmed time and again underscores the importance and centrality of this belief within the Judeo-Christian tradition. In commenting upon Genesis 1:26

through 1:31, and especially on the implications of God's creating humans in the divine image, Charles M. Murphy suggests how humans are meant to interact with other created beings:

> A note of sheer delight on the part of God the Creator can be detected as God proudly surveys his work. Again and again in the creation story God is said to see all that he has made and to pronounce it "very good." Part of that goodness is the natural opulence and generosity of the creation, mirroring in this respect the goodness of the One who made it. In this joyous society the first man and woman occupy a central place, but in continuity with the other creatures which similarly have received sexual differentiation and the blessing of fertility.[3]

Christians maintain that the goodness of creation together with God's immanent presence prompts the belief that creation is a sacrament. The entirety of creation, that is, the universe, or a specific aspect such as a sunset, a distant mountain, the sounds of the ocean, or the silhouette of a deer glimpsed at sunrise are sacraments. The reason they are sacraments is because they allow the divine presence to disclose itself to humans and invite humans to respond spontaneously to God.

Fourth. There is no doubt that dualism is a powerful motif in Christian religious thinking but there are reasons to hope that a recognition of how harmful dualism is will prompt Christians to abandon it. The greatest harm caused by dualism is that it prevents humans from encountering God in the sacrament of creation and from cultivating an appropriate respect for this sacrament. Another harm is that dualism hinders people from esteeming their bodily existence and striving for fulfillment precisely as the whole people they are. The facts that dualism was foreign to Hebrew thought and that they experienced holism in the way they related to nature are the subject of an apropos commentary by Dr. Gloria Thomas:

> For the Israelite nation, God and the world were not at odds. The world and its history were the arena of God's

revelation. The goodness of life, the richness of the earth, and the joy of living as humans were clearly understood as God's blessings. God loved the world . . . throughout the Old Testament, the goodness of the world is praised. Divisions of persons into body and spirit were not part of Jewish understanding. The good human person was not described as a religious person, but as a whole person, free, fulfilled. In Hebrew, there is no word for *psyche* or soul. God was found through living, within life, and this life was to be celebrated. This holistic thinking sustained great love of the family . . . and deep cherishing of the earth and the gifts of nature. Jesus spoke His message upon the foundations of this culture. His parables reflected this understanding. "Look at the lilies of the field, they neither spin nor toil" (Matthew 6:28).[4]

One of the goals of people of faith who resolve to act responsibly toward the environment is to develop an holistic way of thinking and to establish a felt-connectedness to the whole web of life. James Limburg looks to the *second creation account in Genesis* in order to suggest a biblical rationale supportive of such a goal:

The Bible's second creation account begins with Genesis 2:4b. The camera zooms in on one planet, the earth.

. . . This time the story begins with the making of ADAM, a man. "The Lord God formed man (ADAM) of dust from the ground (ADAMAH)." The name of this creature links him to the earth out of which he is made. ADAM is made from ADAMAH. Using Latin derivatives we could say that "the Lord God formed humans from the *humus*" . . . The point is that the name of this creature is a play on the Hebrew word for ground, soil, or earth. The man's name is a reminder of where he came from.

The name ADAM also links this creature to the rest of created life. The trees and the animals are also made out of the ground or ADAMAH (2:9,19). The whole account stresses the interrelatedness of creation. The plants, the animals and human beings are all made from the same raw material.[5]

Fifth. Making the pursuit of asceticism—self-restraint, self-discipline and *mortification*—the main focus of one's spiritual life would be unwise because it would lead to the exclusion of many good and wholesome human experiences. Humans feel happiest and most fulfilled when they enjoy companionship and satisfying pleasures; they instinctively seek out food which appeals to their palates, happy times, comfortable surroundings, and occasions to celebrate. Weary humans often approach the Lord in the hope that he will lead them beside restful waters and refresh them. Seeking satisfaction is a universal human trait and suppressing or denying this trait through an exaggerated asceticism would be an unwise deprivation with which to afflict ourselves. Does this mean, however, that asceticism should not be a part of the life of religious people?

In my opinion there is something to be said in favor of a balanced regime which includes ascetic practices in moderation. I base this opinion on the fact that humans are drawn to evil and overindulgence just as they are drawn to goodness and sensible use. The reason humans experience harmful attractions is because of the universal human proclivity to sin. In their best guise ascetic practices are designed to enable humans to consider and face up to God's dominion over them and to try, with God's help, to rise above their inclination to sin. The intention of the ascetic practices associated with *Lent*, *Yom Kippur* and *Ramadan* is to sharpen a believer's focus on God and to consider God's requirement that people of faith live upright lives. If asceticism is approached from a nondualistic mentality so that the body is not devalued, and if there is no reservation about the goodness, beauty and value of God's creation, there is little likelihood that asceticism will engender environmental apathy.

The development of an aesthetic sense, long encouraged within the Judeo-Christian tradition, could serve as a complement to a healthy asceticism. The aesthetic sense enables humans to be open to and aware of beauty, order, and loveliness in all their manifold forms. Religious people who possess an aesthetic sense are likely to echo the sentiments of the psalmist:

> Lord my God, you are very great,
> clothed in majesty and splendour,
> and enfolded in a robe of light.
>
> You have spread out the heavens like a tent,
> and laid the beams of your dwelling on the waters;
>
> You take the clouds for your chariot,
> riding on the wings of the wind;
> you make the winds your messengers,
> flames of fire your servants;
> you fixed the earth on its foundation
> so that it will never be moved. (Psalm 104:1-5)

People who are moved by the goodness and splendor of nature and who acknowledge all creation as a blessed reflection of God will be inclined to become synchronized with nature. They may even be open to letting God heal them through nature. Anxious, bored, confused, depressed, fatigued or ill they may retreat to the wilderness, the seashore, the mountain top or the glistening lake to commune with God and experience her healing in the beauty and tranquility of nature. Nurturing an aesthetic sense is important for people who endure the pace and stress of the modern metropolis and who fear the health consequences of polluted air and water. It may only be through acting on the insight provided by an aesthetic sense that they will be able to experience well being.

Spirituality is the totality of presuppositions, hopes, dreams, reservations and religious commitments with which a person stands before God and seeks to relate as a person of faith to others. To counteract a burdensome asceticism and to support the flowering of an aesthetic sense people need to fully value God's good earth and their own being. They need also to move beyond individualistic morality and preoccupation with personal sin, seeking to become just, compassionate, celebratory people whose goal is much broader than self-perfection. They should cherish their bodies, their feelings and their imaginations and should desire to become instruments of peace and healing for other humans and for the cosmos as well.

Being in touch with such a positive spirituality and feeling connected with creation gives rise to a religiously-based sense of wonder. Wonder includes elements of marvel and mystery and it is experienced in conjunction with fascination over nature's complexity and a sense of the unfathomable greatness of its creator. Such an insight was expressed in Isaiah:

Do you not know, have you not heard?

The Lord, the eternal God,
creator of earth's farthest bounds,
does not weary and grow faint;
his understanding cannot be fathomed.

He gives vigor to the weary,
new strength to the exhausted.

Young people may grow weary and faint,
even the fittest may stumble and fall;
but those who look to the Lord will win new strength,
they will soar as on eagle's wings;
they will run and not feel faint,
march on and not grow weary.

Sixth. Although the patriarchal-hierarchical-pyramidal way of thinking which has been institutionalized within the Judeo-Christian tradition is defended by male hierarchs and proponents of the status quo as God's will or the best possible governing arrangement, scholarship and common sense reveal that this is simply not so. Jesus, a Jew who is regarded by Christians as God's son and God's perfect revelation, called women and men to live together in peace and freedom. Jesus did not belittle women, use them, or deny them respect, consideration or status. Instead, he ministered to women, healed them, visited them and was himself healed by their faith and their love. Not by any stretch of the imagination could one attribute the oppressive pattern of male domination over women which is an unmistakable part of Christian history to Jesus' will or instructions. Since sexist structures run counter to Jesus' intentions and since they have even been acknowledged by the Roman Catholic bishops of the United States as a sinful aberration[6] there is no question that the churches should divest themselves of sexism. It goes without saying that Rome cannot be changed in a day but that does not mean that a new and better system for church management cannot be devised and implemented.

Feminist thinkers—both women and men—advocate an inclusive and collaborative structure for church government. Feminists demand acknowledgement of women's equality with men and the valuing of women's wisdom and experience within churches and synagogues. Women's experience in respect to ecological consciousness needs especially to be integrated into religious thinking. Women relate easily to the earth: both women and the earth bring forth life and both need to be healthy in order to nurture gestating life and sustain it after birth. Unlike men, women do not tend to define themselves by what they do or to base their morality on abstract principles; rather they define themselves in terms of their relationships and they tend to emphasize the stability of the relationships, networks and webs to which they are committed when they make moral decisions. Women understand life on earth as a whole, a circle, in which, following God's design, each of the millions of species in existence has a part to play. In regard to structures of organization feminists prefer collaboration and consensus to competition and alienation. In regard to nature they advocate adaptation and identification instead of exploitation and destruction rationalized by appeals to human supremacy.

One of the brightest lights in Christendom was Saint Francis of Assisi, the patron saint of the environment. Francis' insight that all creatures are related in the depths of their being by the fact of being creatures[7] led to his beautiful articulation of the communion in God of all beings that share in creaturehood. Francis recognized the sun and moon, earth and air, fire and water, his own body and all animals and plants as brothers and sisters. Francis considered himself and every other mortal to be companions with each other because of their creaturehood. Michael and Kenneth Himes maintain that the notion of companionship might provide the basis for a non-anthropocentric approach to environmental ethics. In this connection they suggest:

The first point of orientation that the companionship motif provides is the desirability of a transformed context within which to develop an environmental ethic. Governed by images of stewardship and ruled by precepts based on self-interest, our moral imaginations are unable to envision an environmental ethic that is adequate to the Jewish and Christian heritage. In contrast, images of companionship encourage the moral imagination to consider more than the good of the individual self is at stake. Once the *intrinsic good* of creation is seen, then approaches to the environmental crisis that treat creation only as an instrumental good to humanity become inadequate.[8]

In summation, the biblical concept of stewardship, properly understood, understands that the care of the earth has been entrusted to humans. Whether or not the entrenchment of the stewardship concept is preventing Christians from articulating a vibrant and imaginative environmental ethics, as the Himes suggest, can only be determined on the basis of extensive dialogue which is just now beginning. In any event, God's charge to protect and nurture fragile forms of life and to look with reverence upon all of creation ought to be received as a blessed gift. Becoming aware of God's presence to creation, how creation reveals the greatness of God, the harms of dualism and the attractiveness of holism, the way wonder and appreciation flow from the aesthetic sense, and the religious and ecological insights conveyed by feminist thinkers can enable the Judeo-Christian tradition to provide a religious foundation for environmental responsibilty.

Does the Judeo-Christian Tradition Need to Abandon Anthropocentrism in order to Become an Effective Voice for Environmental Responsibility?

In my opinion the Judeo-Christian tradition should not abandon what it has always held about the human species in regard to the special giftedness of women and men who are distinguished by the powers of reasoning and will and who are destined to live forever. Therefore, I reject an egalitarian worldview within which all other forms of life are considered equal to humans. The religious worldview I would be inclined to adopt would be a nuanced anthropocentric one. A definition of anthropocentrism which sets the human person at the center of the universe and vests the human with the power and authority to assess the value of all other beings in terms of their usefulness to humans would be rejected. Rather, I would hold that humans have dominion over nature because God entrusted the care of the earth to humankind. God's charge of trusteeship to humans does not mean that humans *own* the earth. It is God who *owns* the earth and humans reside thereon because of God's benevolence. While the things of nature are inspiring and beneficial to humans, they are also pleasing to God and thus are valuable regardless of human opinion because, as Genesis stated, when God looked at them God saw that they were good. It is appropriate, then, for humans to approach the earth with reverence and to base care for nature on nature's wellbeing as well as human present and future need. The self-centeredness which has become a corollary of the stewardship concept needs to be expunged. This might best be accomplished by thinking of humans as grateful, humble users of God's gifts who are called to heal and replenish the earth. Crassness, exploitation and greed need to be exposed as the sins which they are and any assault on the web of life needs to be understood as a crime against the Creator of life.

Religious Insight of Eastern Religions and Native American Religions Contribute to a Sense of Environmental Responsibility

Several insights promotive of ecological sensitivity can be learned from *Eastern religions* which, in contrast to the Judeo-Christian tradition, are neither dualistic nor anthropocentric. Within the Western tradition believers understand themselves as both different and distant from the earth. According to Eastern religious traditions, on the other hand, people consider themselves intimately connected to the earth and they believe that nature is imbued with divinity. The ancient religiously-based morality of the East contains prescriptions about how humans should approach and interact with nature. In contrast the Ten Commandments of the Judeo-Christian tradition only contain directions pertaining to the way humans ought to act toward God and one another. When Buddhists enter into solitude to pray they do not separate themselves from earth and time; instead, they strengthen their connections with all of life. But in being connected to life Buddhists strive not to cling to anything so as to find peace in detachment and freedom.

Thomas Merton (1915-1968), a Trappist monk who traveled to the East to study Buddhism and dialogue with Buddhists, was a prolific writer who exercised and continues to exercise, a significant influence on Western religious thought. Merton discovered that by borrowing some of the religious insight of the East and integrating it into the Christian faith which he professed he became a more content and reverent person. In *New Seeds of Contemplation* he reveals how he perceives nonhuman beings as sharing in the holiness of God:

> The forms and individual characters of living and growing things, of inanimate beings, of animals and flowers and all nature, constitute their holiness in the sight of God. . . . The special clumsy beauty of this particular colt on this April day in these fields under these clouds is a holiness consecrated to God by His own creative wisdom and it declares the glory of God. . . . The pale flowers of the dogwood outside this window are saints. . . . The lakes hidden among the hills are saints. . . . The great, gashed, half naked mountain is another of God's saints.[9]

Native American peoples have an intuitively reverent attitude toward nature. They consider humans and other life forms as constituting a single society and think of themselves as sisters and brothers to every species in the universe. According to the custom of some Native American tribes bears are called Bear People and fish such as salmon are understood as the Salmon Nation. The distinction between Native Americans and the animals and fish to whom they consider themselves related is thus devoid of anthropocentric tendencies, leading to an organic notion of the web of life. The Euro-American practices of land ownership as well as the buying and selling of land are foreign to some Native American tribes. Nature is understood by them as independent or belonging to itself; ownership of nature is considered morally wrong because, by taking ownership, an individual or a group is making a slave of nature.

In 1884 Chief Seattle of the Suquamish tribe gave a moving speech to an assembled group of Indian tribes who were about to sign treaties with white Americans who had taken over their lands. His emotional love for the earth from which the Native American ecological ethic proceeds is evident in his remarks:

> Teach your children . . . that the earth is our mother. What-
> ever befalls the earth befalls the children of the earth. If we
> spit upon the ground, we spit upon ourselves. This we
> know. The earth does not belong to us; we belong to the
> earth. This we know. All things are connected like the
> blood which unites one family. All things are connected.
> Whatever befalls the earth befalls the children of the earth.
> We did not weave the web of life; we are merely a strand in
> it. God is the God of all people, and God's compassion is
> equal for the red and for the white. The earth is precious to
> God, and to harm the earth is to heap contempt on its cre-
> ator. So if we sell you our land, love it as we've loved it.
> Care for it as we've cared for it. Hold in your mind the
> memory of the land as it is when you take it. And with all
> your strength, with all your mind, with all your heart, pre-
> serve it for your children and love it—as God loves us all.
> —Chief Seattle

Thomas Berry admires the ability of Native American people to reach deep into the realms of numinous power and comments on how their nature mysticism is replete with reverence for the earth:

> . . . the Indian peoples of America have their own special
> form of nature mysticism. Awareness of a numinous pres-
> ence throughout the entire cosmic order establishes among
> these people one of the most integral forms of spirituality
> known to us. The cosmos, human, and divine are present
> to one another in a way that is unique. It is difficult to find
> a word or expression for such a mode of experience. It

might simply be called a nature *mysticism*. This is precisely the mystique that is of utmost necessity at the present time to reorient the consciousness of the present occupants of the North American continent toward a reverence for the earth, so urgent if the biosystems of the continent are to survive.[10]

New Perspectives in Christian Theology Suggest Fruitful Approaches to Environmental Responsibility

Theology is faith seeking understanding. We need to give expression to our knowledge of God and, in so doing, we employ terms and categories which are meaningful to us. In my formative years I was introduced to God as a supreme almighty spirit who was infinite, distant and, for me, rather unapproachable. I was not inclined to associate God with the happenings of the world, my life or nature except in a rather remote and dispassionate sense. In sharing faith as an adult I have come to realize that most Christian people who have Judeo-Christian roots held, or still hold, similar notions about God. I have also learned that three new perspectives in Christian theology emphasize other dimensions of God and contribute fruitful religious insight in regard to environmental responsibility.

Process theology understands God not only as transcendent perfect being but also as immanent becoming. Alfred North Whitehead, a philosopher who published seminal works in the 1920s and 1930s, is the architect of process theology. Whitehead proposed that there are two aspects of God: the primordial nature which is the abstract dimension, all-knowing, changeless, unmoved and untouched by any earthly happening, and the consequent nature, through which God is related to the earth and affected by what happens on earth. The consequent God of process theology feels sad when people suffer and rejoices in their happiness. This God is active in the world, availing the world of possibilities for wholeness and growth. She acts as a lure enticing and drawing the earth and humankind to an interactive kind of harmony which aims at the well-being of all. Jesus' words "I have come to give you life, that you might live it to the full" (John 10:10) are seen as the divine will for humans and for all of creation.

Relationality is central to process theology; consider Jay B. McDaniel's comments in this regard:

> In process theology these relations (among organisms) are not abstract spatial properties such as "above" and "below"; they are rather concrete acts of taking into account the other entities from the point of view of the entity as issue. . . .
>
> Relationality also applies in a more general way to communities. A "community" may be an atom, molecule, living cell, animal body, ecosystem, bioregion, or, in its more distinctively human manifestations, a family, neighborhood, town, city, ethnic tradition, or nation . . . The web of life is best conceived as a collective "we" in which, ontologically speaking, there are no "theys."
>
> An inclusive appreciation of the web of life leads to a reverence for life. To revere life is to appreciate the value of living beings for themselves, for one another, *and for God; and it is to recognize that diverse forms of life contribute to the very well-being of God's life.*[11]

Process thought expands the classical doctrine of God to include the dimension of God's becoming. The God of process theology experiences joy, sorrow and uneasiness because of God's interrelationship to the earth and humans. The insights of Teilhard de Chardin, a Jesuit priest who died in 1955, evolved from a lifelong devotion to study and writing focused on *Christology* and science. Teilhard understood the cosmos as constantly evolving, going through stages which he called spheres, and moving inexorably toward culmination in Christ, the Omega point. Teilhard believed that Christ's presence in the universe provides the energy to draw everything to greater consciousness and spiritual awareness. If questions regarding the future of the ecosystem of the earth had been raised in Teilhard's day, I think he would have been optimistic. Teilhard would probably have speculated that by the grace of Christ, who is present to all of creation and who is guiding the evolutionary process, the earth will be healed through its own regenerative powers along with a new human commitment emerging out of a raised consciousness. Recognizing the influence of Christ in the on-going evolution of creation provides a new clue to God's immanence. The influence of the historic Jesus of the bible and Christian tradition can be appreciated alongside the action of the Cosmic Christ in the on-going creation; and creation demands to be apprehended as holy precisely because of Christ's action in it. Since Teilhard's reading of Colossians inspired the development of his Christocentric approach to creation, Colossians (1:15-17; 19-20) may become a fruitful source of religious insight for Christians who are seeking to find a religious basis for environmental responsibility:

> Jesus is the image of the invisible God; his is the primacy over all creation. In him everything in heaven and on earth was created, not only things visible but also the invisible orders of thrones, sovereignties, authorities, and powers; the whole universe has been created through him and for him. He exists before all things, and all things are held together in him. . . . For in him God in all his fullness chose to dwell, and through him to reconcile all things to himself, making peace through the shedding of his blood on the cross—all things, whether on earth or in heaven. (Col.1:15-17; 19-20)

Mohandas K. Gandhi (1869-1948), the leader in the movement for Indian independence once said, "There is enough for everyone's need but not for everyone's greed." Liberation theology developed in Latin America in the 1960s and 1970s because of a felt religious need to respond to a situation in which the basic human needs of millions of people went unmet while a small aristocratic class grew constantly more wealthy. Large numbers of both the rich and poor were Catholic Christians; yet there was a centuries old entrenched tradition in which the rich were indifferent to the needs of the poor and the poor were fatalistic in accepting the status quo. Liberation theology is unique in that it responded to this situation by beginning with the gospels and the experience of the poor. Gathered in small communities the poor of Latin America reflect on the scriptures and their experience and work from the foundation they create to try to improve their economic and spiritual lives. Liberation theology exposes the harm done by abusive, exploitative and oppressive forces and refuses to allow that harm to continue. By applying the strategy of liberation theology to environmental issues people who are concerned for the earth's well-being will find a means to resist and overcome the assaults of greedy and powerful people upon the land.

Environmental Responsibility and the Exercise of Prophetic Ministry

Some religious believers are not aware that the earth is endangered. Others have heard that the earth is endangered but still they manage to ignore the situation. Fortunately there are some people of faith who are both aware of environmental dangers and active in the work of healing the earth. Those who link faith with an ecological consciousness and speak for the earth, educate others in environmental responsibility or organize efforts to restore the earth's integrity fulfill a prophetic ministry, that is, they convey God's will in respect to her creation. The Old Testament contains sixteen prophetic books which record exhortations, admonitions or reassuring messages directed to the Hebrew people by spokespersons for God. In recent years the messages of such environmental prophets as Thomas Berry and H. Paul Santmire[12] have borne much fruit. There are many other prophets throughout the world known only to their local communities. It is difficult to pay sufficient credit to the importance of the efforts of religiously-motivated individuals and groups on behalf of the environment. The time is at hand, however, for church leadership to enthusiastically embrace the challenge to speak on behalf of environmental responsibility.

The Roman Catholic Church has a one-hundred-year-old tradition of social ethical teaching. Ever since the issuance of the *encyclical Rerum Novarum* ("On the Condition of Labor") by Pope Leo XIII in 1891, popes and national councils of bishops have addressed a wide range of social-ethical issues and offered their analyses to Catholic Christians and the wider community for consideration. Two recent *pastoral letters* by the Catholic bishops of the United States dealing with the nuclear danger and economic injustice[13] were well received and prompted extensive discussion. It goes without saying that it is past time for Catholic leaders to address environmental responsibility, establishing appropriate religious linkages.

There are four reasons to anticipate that Catholic leadership will develop a comprehensive response to the environmental crisis.

First. The Catholic Church has consistently spoken out in defense of the rights and dignity of the human person, being an advocate for those who suffer from economic, political or religious oppression. In recent years token attention has also been paid to racism and sexism. Extending Catholic social teaching to the tragic effects on people of famines, coastal flooding and the poisoning of land, air and waters would represent a natural progression. Although unquestionably anthropocentric in orientation, any forthcoming teaching would likely be uncompromising about the human responsibility to heal the earth.

Second. Catholic moral teaching has taken account of increasingly more complex economic and political systems by becoming more subtle and tentative in its analyses. Accordingly, in 1891, *Rerum Novarum* argued simply that working persons have the right to join unions and receive a "living wage" while performing a fair day's work. Eighty years later in 1971 Pope Paul VI explored in *Octagesima Adveniens* ("A Call to Action") how power might be exercised by political leaders so as to obtain economic justice for those in need. Paul VI, recognizing the differences and complexities within and among societies, resisted the temptation to suggest a solution which would have "universal validity." Instead he counseled communities and nations to engage in dialogue to determine an approach which might be appropriate for them. On December 30, 1987, Pope John Paul II issued the encyclical *Sollicitudo Rei Socialis* ("On Social Concern"). In it John Paul engaged in the most sophisticated analysis to date of the political tensions in the world and their connection to the social and economic deprivation of people. "John Paul II made clear that the Church was not in a position to propose a third approach to economic, political and social organization as an alternative to Marxism and capitalism. Instead the pope defined the Church's task as that of presenting 'a careful reflection on the complex realities of human existence, in society and in the international order, in the light of faith and of the Church's tradition.'"[14]   Because Catholic leadership engages life on earth precisely as a "complex reality" there is reason to believe that they will be open to taking all relevant factors into consideration when they formulate a comprehensive teaching on the environment.

Third. Pope John Paul II has already begun to integrate environmental concerns into his teachings. In *Sollicitudo Rei Socialis* he wrote about "the need to respect the integrity and cycles of nature and to take them into account when planning for development."[15] The pope went on to reaffirm the superior status given to humans but cautioned that humans "must remain subject to the will of God, who imposes limits upon use and dominion over things."[16] John Paul II also warned his readers that when humans disobey God and refuse to submit to God's rule, nature rebels against them, no longer recognizing human mastery because the divine image in the human becomes tarnished.[17] The pope's own evolving ecological consciousness is also given expression:

> One cannot use with impunity the different categories of beings . . . simply as one wishes, according to one's own economic needs. On the contrary, one must take into account *the nature of each being* and of its *mutual connection* in an ordered system which is precisely the "cosmos."[18]

He goes on to counsel wise use of nonrenewable natural resources and warn about the serious health consequences associated with pollution.

In the World Day of Peace message of January 1, 1990 John Paul II clearly placed the blame for environmental degradation in human hands. He enjoined his audience to accept responsibility for the care of the earth:

> The increasing devastation of the world of nature results from the behavior of people who show a callous disregard for the hidden, yet perceivable requirements of the order and harmony which govern nature itself.
>
> An adequate solution cannot be found merely in a better management or a more rational use of earth's resources; it

must go to the source of the problem and face that more profound moral crisis of which the environment is only one aspect.

The environmental crisis is a moral crisis. It is not simply an accident or an unavoidable coincidence. We humans have to accept responsibility for the bad choices we have made.[19]

Fourth. The Philippine bishops issued a pastoral letter entitled "What Is Happening to Our Beautiful Land?" on January 29, 1988. Sensitive, emotional, reverent and inspiring, its tone is a decided improvement in Catholic *episcopal teaching.* The Philippine bishops speak from their hearts to their people about the fear and sadness they feel when they behold the damaged environment of their country:

Our forests laid waste

How much of this richness and beauty is left a few thousand years after human beings arrived at these shores? Look around and see where our forests have gone. Out of the original 30 million hectares there is now only 1 million hectares of primary forest left. Where are some of the most beautiful creatures who used to dwell in our forests? These are God's masterpieces, through which he displays his power, ingenuity and love for his creation. Humans have forgotten to live peacefully with other creatures. They have destroyed their habitat and hunted them relentlessly. Even now many species are already extinct and the destruction of species is expected to increase dramatically during the next decade as the few remaining stands of forest are wiped out by loggers and kaingineros. What about the birds? They used to greet us each morning and lift our spirits beyond the horizons of this world. Now they are silenced. In many places all we hear now are cocks crowing. Where is the soaring eagle circling above the land or the colorful kalaw (hornbill)?

The hemorrhage of our life blood

After a single night's rain look at the chocolate brown rivers in your locality and remember that they are carrying the life blood of the land into the sea. The soil, instead of being the seed bed of life, becomes a cloak of death, smothering, retarding and killing coral polyps. Soil specialists tell us that we lose the equivalent of 100,000 hectares of soil one meter thick each year. We are hardly aware of this enormous loss which is progressively eroding away our most fertile soil and thus our ability to produce food for an expanding population. Any comprehensive land reform must address this most serious threat to our food supply.

Deserts in the sea

How can fish swim in running sewers like the Pasig and so many more rivers which we have polluted? Who has turned the wonderworld of the seas into underwater cemeteries bereft of color and life? Imagine: only 5 per cent of our corals are in their pristine state! The blast of dynamite can still be heard on our coastal waters. We still allow *muro-ami* fishing methods which take a terrible toll both on the young swimmers and the corals. Mine tailings are dumped into fertile seas like Calancan Bay where they destroy forever the habitat of the fish. Chemicals are poisoning our lands and rivers. They kill vital organisms and in time they will poison us. The ghost of the dreaded Minamata disease hangs over towns in the Agusan river basin and the Davao gulf.[20]

The Philippine bishops go on to include themselves in the work of restoration: "As Filipinos we can and must act now. This is our home; we must care for it, watch over it, protect it and love it. We must be particularly careful to protect what remains of our forests, rivers, and corals and to heal, wherever we can, the damage which has already been done." I suspect that simple eloquent passion expressed by religious leaders like those in the Philippines may have more motivational power than the tedious, abstract, theoretical treatises which are the staple of religious leaders.

A Stumbling Block

A stumbling block which Catholic leadership faces in regard to formulating a rationally adequate position on environmental responsibility consists in speaking with credibility on the issue of population growth. Even if pollution is brought under control, how many mouths can the earth feed? For how many people can the earth provide healthy habitats? There is no simple answer to complex questions like these. Responding, however, that God will provide sustenance for whatever number of humans inhabit the earth in the future would represent an inexcusable evasion of hierarchical responsibility. This evasion would be made more grievous if it were based on a reluctance to reexamine the hierarchical ban on artificial contraception in light of relevant environmental data.

Conclusion

In order to formulate a religiously-inspired response to our endangered planet we need to get beyond dualistic attitudes which are tolerant of various forms of oppression and which lead to the disparagement of the earth. We need to cultivate a reverent attitude toward creation, the work of God's hands. And we ought to develop a sense of appreciation for the beauty and order of the cosmos along with a heartfelt commitment to healing the wounded earth. We should be open to the teachings and insights of all religious traditions concerning the holiness of the earth.

Imagining a traveler looking down from a remote pass in the Himalayas, St. Francis of Assisi wrote a meditation; from it we need to learn above all to move beyond self-absorbed individualism to a deep and profound awareness of the connectedness of all beings within the web of life:

> High up in the mounts far distant from any human habitation he will think of humanity below, struggling, panting, sorrowing, rejoicing, always somewhere tilling the soil, somewhere sowing seed, somewhere reaping the harvest, somewhere gathering fruits, tending flock and herds, building habitations, enjoying social intercourse, making love,

bearing children, seeking the Truth, making beauty, worshipping God. But the traveler will not think of men as separate individuals. Mankind will be to him as one and as organically connected with that Nature he sees spread before him.[21]

Exercise

Marie Wilson is a Native American who resides in British Columbia and is a member of the Gitksan Tribe. In an interview conducted by the authors of *The New Catalyst* she explains some aspects of Gitksan philosophy. Consider the questions posed and the answers given:

TNC: So you don't take a stewardship perspective to the land—in the sense that the land needs our protection?

Marie Wilson: Oh, never! No, the land can do what it will with me. We cannot whip the waves back. When the waves come, they can strip the California beach of million dollar homes in one contemptuous wave.

TNC: . . . Do you have any advice for non-Indian people who are struggling for their vision?

Marie Wilson: In Gitksan society, before you became adult enough to take on responsibility and power, you went out alone. Alone, we search for our full potential. After fasting for days and going into the sweat lodge and the cold waters of the stream, whipping oneself with the Devil's Club, I imagine we were in a fine state of hallucination. We had visions, usually in the form of a creature, or an encounter with a natural resource like the sun. The intention was not necessarily to find the creature but rather our own full potential.

When people fast, their bodies are reverting to the survival mode of existence where only that which is absolutely necessary is being taken from the body itself. This is going back to the natural Gitksan: taking only what is required. Our territories are taken for need, not greed. We take creatures for need, never more than we can use. When the body is in this state, fasting is not at all painful. You are then able to reach this perception where smell, touch, taste take on a fresh sensitivity. Not only these things, but also an increased perception of my place, my home, my children. So, imagine what happened to our people when they fasted for days. They became so empty that they were like snow in the spring—melting water drips through the snow and it becomes porous. This must have been the condition they were in—ready to receive.

The Gitksan accepted their intelligence for what it was, as they accepted their wonderful bodies.

TNC: We have to rediscover this intelligence. My concern has been that non-Indian people have the tendency to think that we can have it all now; there it is, over there in that native culture, I'll just go and take it. We can't do that.

Marie Wilson: That's right. There's no way non-Indian people can really understand the emotion, the sense of defeat and elation, the way we've had to change our attitudes as we learned. None of this shows up. This has taken thousands of years for us to come to this point.

TNC: What do we do then? As people who are desperate for this meaning?

Marie Wilson: You will have to go back in your own history, as many Gitksan have had to do. We are drowning in statistics and yet we are aching for this knowledge.[22]

• How would you respond to someone who speaks disparagingly of Native American cultures as "primitive"?

• In what kind of a process might you engage to find your "full potential"?

• What do you require for physical, emotional and spiritual well-being?

• Do you think that you can take what you are lacking from another culture so that you will become complete?

• If it has taken the Gitksan thousands of years to come to the wise belief that territories should be taken for need, not greed, how long will it take Euro-Americans to get beyond their greed?

• What kind of knowledge must people of the Judeo-Christian tradition seek in order to live in harmony with the earth?

• Comment on the complexities and difficulties attendant to establishing attitudes which are characterized by respect and reverence for the earth.

Questions for Discussion

1. Canvass the houses of worship in your community and speak with the persons in charge of religious education. Inquire as to how the relationships between God and creation and between humans and creation are understood within each faith tradition. Ask about any programs which might be in place (or in the planning phase) which stress human responsibility for the earth. Prepare a five minute oral report or a two page written report on what you learn.

2. Identify the dualisms which you may have integrated into your thinking as a result of your religious upbringing. Do you consider your personal dualistic attitudes an asset or a drawback? If you see them as a drawback, what steps could you take to change them?

3. Define monotheism, pantheism, panentheism, immanence, transcendence, eschatology, sacrament, dualism, holism, asceticism, the aesthetic sense, patriarchy and feminism. Write a sentence using each term which makes a connection between the term used and the goal of a religiously-derived sense of environmental responsibility.

4. Explain how people whose faith is rooted in the Judeo-Christian tradition might learn from the bible to respect, value and love nature.

5. List four religious insights which Eastern religions and Native American traditions offer in regard to respect for the environment.

6. What do process theologians mean by the consequent nature of God? Describe your reaction to the possibility of God's experiencing joy or sadness because of what happens to her creation or her children.

7. If you are a Christian, in what manner are you accustomed to thinking of Jesus? Did it ever occur to you to think of Jesus as Teilhard de Chardin did, as the Cosmic Christ? How would your faith be altered if you were to add to it the insight that Jesus is the Cosmic Christ?

8. If you were to write a letter to a religious leader requesting that he or she develop a religiously-based church teaching on environmental responsibility, state five points which you would make in your letter.

9. Compose a hymn or prayer addressed to God expressing human need for God's help in the task of healing the earth.

Debate

Resolved: In the interest of promoting the sustainability of the earth through preventing overpopulation by humans the hierarchical leadership of the Roman Catholic Church should abandon its teaching in opposition to artificial contraception and adopt a position advocating this practice.

For Further Reading

Thomas Berry, *The Dream of the Earth* (San Francisco: Sierra Book Club, 1988).

Eileen Flynn and Gloria Thomas, *Living Faith: An Introduction to Theology* (Kansas City: Sheed & Ward, 1988).

Sean McDonagh, SSC, *The Greening of the Church* (Maryknoll, NY: Orbis Books, 1990).

Roderick Frazier Nash, *The Rights of Nature* (Madison, Wisc.: The University of Wisconsin Press, 1989), Chapter 4.

H. Paul Santmire, *The Travail of Nature* (Philadelphia: Fortress, 1985).

Glossary

Author of Genesis 1:26: The person (or persons) who first described creation by God over six days with the seventh day given to sabbath rest is unknown. Authorship of Genesis 1:1-2:4a is attributed by scholars to a person or group known as the Priestly author because of his (their) commitment to radical monotheism as well as temple formulas and rituals, two primary concerns of the Israelite priestly clan.

Christology: The study of who Jesus was, that is, the historical Jesus about whom we learn in the bible. Also, the study of Jesus' presence to believers and Jesus' ongoing activity in creation as the Cosmic Christ. Teilhard de Chardin's, *The Phenomenon of Man* (New York: Harper and Row, 1959) is a good source for an introduction to the Cosmic Christ.

Concept of God: The way a person thinks of God, her idea or notion of who God is, e.g., a golden calf, an elderly bearded man robed in white and sitting on a cloud, a stern judge, or a compassionate mother embracing her child.

Eastern Religions: Such approaches to gods, God, faith, and worship as are embodied in Buddhism, Hinduism, Jainism, Shinto, Taoism, Zen Buddhism.

Encyclical: A letter written by or for a pope which is addressed to all Catholics and people of good will which contains Catholic teaching on a specific subject such as artificial birth control or peace in the modern world. Encyclicals are identified by their first two or three Latin words.

Episcopal Teaching: The teaching of national councils of Roman Catholic bishops, by themselves or in union with other councils. Another name for the office held by bishops is the episcopate.

Eschatology: The study of the final things, that is, death, judgment, heaven and hell. An eschatological outlook tends to consider the importance of events and experience in relation to the ultimate importance of the final things.

Immanent: Close, near, within.

Intrinsic Good: Good in itself regardless of whether it has any usefulness to anything or anyone. A flower which blooms and dies unseen could be said to have intrinsic goodness or worth because it pleases God, or simply because it is a lovely thing which exists for a time.

Judeo-Christian Tradition: The heritage of faith, principles and wisdom which Christians value. This tradition begins with the role played by Abraham approximately two thousand years before the birth of Christ and continues to the present time.

Lent: The forty-day season of renewal and penance preceding Easter, the celebration of the Resurrection.

Mortification: A penitential practice such as self-denial or fasting designed to cause the death of evil inclinations. (*Mors* means death, and *facere* means to make.)

Mysticism: Experiencing God's presence in a very intense way; approaching God as a divine person who wants to establish an intimate relationship with believers.

Native American Religions: The rituals, celebrations and beliefs of the native inhabitants of the American continents which approached the entire ecosystem as sacred.

Noncorporeality: According to the Judeo-Christian tradition, God's condition of being a pure spirit and having no body, thus being neither male nor female.

Pastoral Letters: Statements of faith, morality or policy written by single bishops or groups of bishops to apprise their followers and the members of the larger society on some aspect of teaching.

Pre-Patriarchal Religions: Those matriarchal and polytheistic religions which people followed (and, in some places still follow) before the establishment of the Judeo-Christian tradition.

Ramadan: A month during which Muslims fast during daylight hours as well as refrain from smoking, sex, injections and the intake of fragrances.

Second Creation Account in Genesis: Genesis 2:4b-24 is believed by scholars to be the work of an author or authors known as the Yahwist because God is referred to as Yahweh. In this account God is depicted as creating the male human from the earth and his female companion from the male's rib.

Theologians: Women and men who serve their faith communities by studying scripture and tradition, by dialoguing among themselves and with the members of the broader community, and by presenting oral and written commentaries on faith and religion.

Transcendent: When posited of God, to be above and infinitely superior to all creation, but not to imply that God is distant from or unconcerned about humans.

Yom Kippur: The Jewish day of atonement is the strictest day in the year for Jewish people. Most Jews, both religious and nonreligious, observe Yom Kippur by fasting and abstaining from sex and bathing and by not wearing leather shoes.

End Notes

1. Lynn White, Jr., "The Historical Roots of Our Ecological Crisis," *Science*, 155:3767, March 10, 1967, pp. 1203-1207.

2. Cf., Andrew Christiansen, S.J., "Ecology, Justice, and Development," *Theological Studies*, 51:1, March, 1990, pp. 71-72, especially note 22.

3. Charles M. Murphy, *At Home On Earth* (New York: Crossroad, 1989) p. 89.

4. Eileen Flynn and Gloria Thomas, *Living Faith: An Introduction to Theology* (Kansas City: Sheed & Ward, 1989), p. 272.

5. James Limburg, "Reflections on the Bible and the Care of the Earth," *The Catholic World*, 233:1396, July/August, 1990, pp. 150, 151.

6. Cf., two drafts of pastoral statements on women's concerns. *Partners in the Mystery of Redemption and One in Christ Jesus*, (Washington: USCC, 1988 and 1990).

7. Michael J. Himes and Kenneth R. Himes, "The Sacrament of Creation," *Commonweal*, CXVII:2, January 26, 1990, p. 45.

8. p. 46.

9. Thomas Merton, *New Seeds of Contemplation* (New York: New Directions, 1972), p. 30.

10. Thomas Berry, *The Dream of the Earth* (San Francisco: Sierra Club Books, 1990), p. 184.

11. Jay B. McDaniel, *Earth, Sky, Gods, and Mortals* (Mystic, Ct.: Twenty Third Publications, 1990), pp. 27, 28.

12. Thomas Berry, an historian of cultures, is a former president of the American Teilhard Association and is the founder and director of the Riverdale Center for Religious Research. A "geologian" Berry's lectures and writing have challenged people to recognize and respect the sacrality of nature.

H. Paul Santmire, the recipient of a doctorate in divinity from Harvard in 1966, authored *The Travail of Nature* (Philadelphia: Fortress, 1985) in which he argued that nature is a full participant in the process of creation and redemption, enlarging upon the notion that it is humans who have been redeemed by Christ.

13. Cf., *The Challenge of Peace and Economic Justice for All* (Washington, DC: USCC, 1983 and 1986).

14. Flynn and Thomas, p. 321.

15. John Paul II, *Sollicitudo Rei Socialis* (Washington, DC: USCC, 1988), 26.

16. 29.

17. 30.

18. 34.

19. John Paul II, "Peace with God the Creator: Peace with All of Creation," in *The Woodstock Report*, 21, March, 1990, p. 10.

20. Philippine Bishops, *What Is Happening to Our Beautiful Land?* as quoted in Sean McDonagh, SSC, *The Greening of the Church* (Maryknoll, NY: Orbis Books, 1990), p. 210.

21. Meditation of Saint Francis, as quoted in "Interfaith Dialogue: A Tradition at Oxford University," *Shared Vision*, 2, Spring, 1988, p. 5.

22. Christopher Plant and Judith Plant, *Turtle Talk* (Philadelphia: New Society, 1990), pp. 83, 84.

Chapter Four

Business, Government and the Environment

Introduction

When considering how business and government should function vis-à-vis the environment, at least two approaches suggest themselves. The first considers the activities of businesses in industrialized societies together with the difficulties encountered by governments in effectively regulating these activities as the major cause of environmental degradation. Because little hope is attached to the possibility of reversing or controlling the harms industry visits on the environment a suggestion is made to move to a post-industrial society. This society would be characterized by a back to the land ethic through which people would seek to live in harmony with their region's ecosystem. Bureaucratic government from the distance would be shunned in favor of the autonomy and self-government of local communities. There would be no belching smoke stacks, little or no reliance on automobiles and consumerism and materialism would be held in disdain. Proponents of a back to the land ethic think that there is still sufficient time to establish this lifestyle. They warn that if industrial pollution continues unabated for years to come the option will be lost because the earth will become uninhabitable.

While changing to a simple agrarian lifestyle sounds appealing, I am sceptical about the possibility of transforming a nation as populous and as economically dependent on industry as the United States into hundreds of thousands of communities organized around consensus government, vegetable patches and cottage industries. I therefore think that the proposal to deindustrialize technologically advanced societies is utopian and impractical; hence, environmental concerns notwithstanding, another approach ought to be adopted. I take this approach with the hope that there is enough time to implement needed reforms.

The second approach consists in reforming industrialized societies so that environmental damage is lessened or eliminated. Realizing that business functions in a secular zone where the operative philosophy is *pragmatism* does not negate the importance of the ethical and religious considerations which were examined in Chapters 2 and 3. It does, however, force us to move beyond theoretical substrata which are not part of the articulated business ethos in order to suggest a practical plan which will be acceptable to the business community. The same criterion of practicality will be advocated in regard to the government's proactive role in legislating and enforcing laws.

Developing a Corporate Conscience

Kenneth E. Goodpaster, the David Koch Professor of Ethics and Corporate Leadership at the College of St. Thomas in St. Paul, Minnesota, said that "Corporations are today more than ever before open to the suggestion that they need a conscience as much as they need a strategy."[1] Two fundamental distinctions need to be made before a corporate conscience can be formed:

> Corporations must distinguish the concept of conscience from its "counterfeits" (public and government relations, competitive strategy, a marketing orientation, legal compliance, and issues management); and management must move to "orient, institutionalize and sustain" the conscience in ways that are as realistic as those that guide strategy formulations and implementation."[2]

According to Goodpaster, exercising conscience entails a three-step process: the first phase entails perception, the middle phase consists of analysis, synthesis and choice, and the final phase focuses on action and evaluation.

During the perception phase salient facts are considered. These include who the appropriate decision-makers are and what the main options are along with the long and short term implications of each option. The next phase requires that the decision-maker determine the pros and cons of each option as well as how each option is likely to affect the environment. In executing the synthesis step, the decision-maker needs to resolve tensions between self-interest and concern for others and needs to decide how to express appropriate care for each of the parties involved. In conjunction with this process the decision-maker cannot help but empathize with stakeholders such as stockholders, employees, suppliers, customers, the public and the environment. Making a choice requires that a particular plan of action be put into place, with due concern given to the manner in which the decision is implemented. Finally, the decision-maker should remain open to reevaluation of the entire process and be willing to deal with problematic aspects of its implementation. It may also be necessary to adopt an entirely new approach or a modified version of the original approach if the original approach does not work out according to expectations.

An example of the exercise of corporate conscience might consist in the realization by the *CEO* of a small petroleum company in light of several highly publicized recent incidents, of the possibility of an oil spill resulting from negligence on the part of a ship's commander who is under the influence of drugs or alcohol. The CEO knows that she has the responsibility of addressing this potential problem. She sees her options as doing nothing other than what she is required by law to do, putting in place a superficial safety program, or initiating a thorough review of existing procedures along with the establishment of a supplemental training program with the offer of confidential counseling about substance abuse and other personal problems for all commanders. The short term implications of doing nothing would be that no money would be spent and no time taken from other management responsibilities; instituting a superficial safety program would cost little in terms of money and time. Putting in place a thorough review of procedures, a comprehensive on the job training program and optional counseling would require a considerable amount of oversight and would be expensive. In terms of the long run, there could be a public relations price to pay for doing nothing, but paying either superficial or thorough attention to the problem could result in a PR benefit. The other long term benefit is that a comprehensive educational program coupled with confidential counseling would be the approach most likely to result in a substance free commander acting responsibly at the helm. In analyzing the pros and cons of each option as well as the possible consequences for the environment, the CEO would necessarily consider the well-being of the waters on which transoceanic oil tankers travel and the harms suffered by marine life from recent oil spills. Within the context of the synthesis step the CEO needs to take account of such factors as her reputation, the requirement to maximize earnings for stockholders, corporate responsibilities to employees, the long-term costs of bad publicity should there be a spill, corporate integrity and the integrity of the oceans and other waterways. It is apparent that only one specific strategy can be put in place. As a result of the analysis associated with the introspective process of synthesizing, the CEO cannot help but develop empathy toward the many constituencies she is charged with serving, not least of which is the environment. If the CEO chooses to provide extensive training and offer counseling, she needs to stay abreast of developments as the program unfolds. If the program is successful, the CEO should try to ascertain why it works. If, in spite of the program, there is evidence that commanders sometimes operate ships while under the influence of narcotics or alcohol, and/or there are oil spills due to negligence, the CEO may need to revamp or replace the program.

This example illustrates the complexity attendant to the exercise of corporate conscience. The CEO of a corporation is responsible to many stakeholders. Including the environment among the enumerated stakeholders is consistent with ecological consciousness as well as reality. To think that the environment should be the first, the only or the most pressing concern of the CEO is probably unrealistic in terms of the facts of life of the corporate world. But making environmental awareness an inherent concern in the exercise of corporate conscience, along with the conviction that it is morally right to exercise care for the earth, constitutes a significant step in the right direction.

Dealing with Industrial Pollution and Waste

The two main sources of air pollution are the smokestack and the auto exhaust, both of which are integral components of industrialized societies. The polluted air we breathe threatens human health. Ozone depletion and global warming are caused by chemical air pollutants; as you will recall from Chapter 1, should these phenomena continue unchecked, disastrous consequences will follow. Acid rain, which returns toxic particulates to earth in liquid form, is already wreaking havoc in lakes and forests.

The earth itself can become polluted through the actions of industry. Agribusiness, which we will consider in a later section of this chapter, is a primary source of this kind of pollution. Careless disposal of toxic substances (as happened at Love Canal) as well as application of poisonous chemicals to the land (as happened at Times Beach) can also pollute the earth.

Oil spills are a blatant example of water pollution. When industries discharge chemical wastes into rivers, oceans or other waterways the resultant pollution is apt to receive little or no media attention but it causes deleterious effects to marine life and frequently to humans as well. Sodium-based substances increase the salinity of water, resulting in the death of fish. When acid-tainted water from mining and milling operations is flushed into rivers and streams, it is lethal to marine life. Phosphorus compounds, used for both domestic and industrial cleaning, cause explosive expansion of algae, which destroy oxygen supplies required by aquatic life. If mercury, a by-product of fossil fuel combustion and paper mill processes, is discharged into a body of water, it will work its way up the food chain, eventually presenting serious health hazards to humans. The cadmium which remains after the manufacture of zinc or which leaks from discarded batteries can make its way into bodies of water and eventually cause such harms as bone disease, cramps, vomiting, diarrhea, high blood pressure and heart disease. Heated water, discharged by industrial pipelines, raises the temperatures of those rivers and streams into which it is discharged, decreasing their ability to hold dissolved oxygen, thus placing oxygen-dependent marine life in peril. Another serious water pollution threat comes from leakage of containerized intermediate and low level radioactive wastes and hazardous chemical wastes which were dumped on the ocean floor and which contaminate the marine food chain.

It should be noted that since 1972 all industrial point source water discharges have been subject to federal and/or state permits in order to limit unsafe levels of discharges. Where these laws have been observed or enforced pollution of waters has been lessened or eliminated. In cases where observance and/or enforcement have not occurred industrial pollution of waters has continued to the detriment of the environment.

In view of the pervasiveness of industrial pollution as well as the harms it causes it is apparent that something should be done about it. But *what* should be done, and *why* should action be taken? Proposing that we clean everything up right away and return nature to its original pristine state would honor the theory that nature is vested with intrinsic worth but it is probably unrealistic because it does not take account of the way our economy is structured. Reaching an accommodation with industry in which a carefully limited amount of pollution is tolerated within a perspective which is concerned for the overall well-being of the earth, while decidedly anthropocentric, is probably the only practical approach. If limits were imposed on industry forbidding the discharge of more pollutants than the earth is capable of absorbing and if the allowable risk to humans were acceptably low, such an accommodation might be feasible. The difficulty with such an approach would be to make sure that industry not try to shirk its responsibilities by finding loopholes that would enable it to evade strict guidelines.

An innovative approach to pollution control calls for reducing or eliminating pollutants at their source or applying technology in creative ways to the pollution problem. The Resource Conservation and Recovery Act of 1976 set the stage for these initiatives by requiring recycling or the reduction of potential wastes at the outset of the process. In regard to minimizing pollutants at their source Manuel G. Velasquez writes:

The technology for pollution control has developed effective but costly methods for abating pollution. Up to 60 percent of water pollutants can be removed through "primary" screening and sedimentation processes; up to 90 percent can be removed through more expensive "secondary" biological and chemical processes; and amounts over 95 percent can be removed through even more expensive "tertiary" chemical treatment. Air pollution abatement techniques include: the use of fuels and combustion procedures that burn more cleanly; mechanical filters that screen or isolate dust particles in the air; "scrubbing" processes that pass polluted air through liquids that remove pollutants; and chemical treatment that transforms gases into more easily removed compounds.[3]

Applying technology in creative ways so as to insure the safe disposal of pollutants and finding non-toxic substances which can be substituted for toxic pollutants are some of the other ways through which industry is attempting to deal wiith pollution. Researchers at the Rocky Flats, Colorado nuclear weapons plant have designed a method for disposal of hazardous nuclear wastes which may also be applicable outside the nuclear industry for industries that generate metal-bearing waste. The new method employs microwaves to heat sludge-type waste to temperatures as high as 2800 degrees Fahrenheit. The waste's moisture content is reduced from about 70 percent to about 20 percent. After the sludge dries, it is mixed with glass-making material. Officials at Rock Flats think that the volume will finally be reduced by four-fifths. At the end of the process the shrunken waste will be encased in glass and stored.[4] (The reader should be aware that in spite of the potential benefits of this particular technology developed by researchers at Rocky Flats that Rocky Flats is perhaps the worst-run nuclear weapons facility in the country and that, over all, the Rocky Flats environmental record is a dismal one.)

At Polaroid Corporation all 1,400 chemicals used in instant photography were recently catalogued and ranked in four categories. A five-year plan with two goals was then put in place: to reduce use of the least toxic materials and to completely eliminate use of all chemicals which were ranked in the worst two categories. Polaroid's articulated commitment is to close the gap between the desire for instant results and the time it actually takes to make things happen.[5]

On July 10,1990 United Parcel Service announced that it planned to convert its 2,700 delivery trucks in Los Angeles to natural gas over a five year period. The reason for switching to natural gas is to comply with anti-smog rules so as to reduce the amount of pollution in smog-choked Los Angeles. "Siro De Gasperis, a vice president of United Parcel, said the company eventually plans to convert to natural gas all its trucks in cities with air problems. He said such a shift would involve about half the company's total fleet of 100,000 distinctive brown trucks."[6]

Modifying the traditional approach to loading oil tankers is suggested as a measure to take in order to prevent oil leaks. The rationale behind this preventive strategy is as follows:

> Some engineers advocate loading tankers less than full—to about 80 percent of capacity—as a ready way to reduce oil spills without modifying tankers. The strategy called hydrostatic balancing, works on a simple principle. Oil gushes from torn ships only so long as the pressure of the oil against the inside of the ship is greater than the water pressure against the outside. When enough oil has escaped so that the pressures are about equal, the hemorrhaging stops—even if millions of gallons remain aboard a badly damaged vessel, as was the case with the Exxon Valdez. So the less full the tanker is to begin with, the less pressure on its internal walls and the less oil rushes into the sea when the hull is ruptured. To keep a less-than-full tanker from riding too high in the ocean, the ballast tanks could be kept permanently filled with water, a departure from the common practice of emptying them as oil is pumped aboard and refilling them as oil is off-loaded. Proponents say this would bring an extra advantage: ship owners could afford to use expensive fresh water if they had to fill the ballast tanks just once, and this would significantly reduce the corrosion caused by the repeated pumping of salt water into and out of the tanks.[7]

The DuPont Company announced on June 22, 1990 that it was building four plants which would be equipped to produce environmentally friendly refrigerants. According to an article written by John Holuska:

> The company said the new plants would produce four types of hydrofluorocarbons, or HFCs, for use in automotive air-conditioners, home refrigerators and commercial refrigeration equipment. The new compounds contain no chlorine and are therefore not expected to pose a threat to the ozone layer.[8]

The cost to DuPont of replacing CFCs was expected to reach $240 million by the end of 1990; total expenditures by the end of the century could exceed $1 billion.[9]

The overall goal of reducing industrial pollution needs to be combined with the design of an industrial ecosystem in which "the use of energy and materials is optimized, wastes and pollution are minimized and there is an economically viable role for every product of a manufacturing process."[10] Ideally, engineers should study how to recover energy from otherwise polluting waste and develop refuse-derived fuel from these wastes. In this way chemicals which would be pollutants outside the industrial complex could serve a useful function within it.

Another innovative approach to the wastes generated in industrial processes is to develop uses for them or to sell them to other industries which could use them. "For example, Meridian National in Ohio, a midwestern steel-processing company, reprocesses the sulfuric acid with which it removes scale from steel sheets and slabs, reuses the acid and sells ferrous sulfate compounds to magnetic-tape manufacturers."[11]

People who design and carry out industrial processes are in the front lines of the war against pollution. Workers will be most inclined to speak up about possible or actual discharge of pollutants if they know that the corporation which employs them is committed to environmental responsibility. At the very least the ethical norm prescribing that no avoidable harm be done to people should be the subject of universal agreement. In light of the most tragic industrial accident in recent years, the December 2, 1984 escape of poisonous gas from the Union Carbide plant in Bhopal, India which caused the deaths of more than 3,500 people and more than 45,000 serious injuries, the gravity of this responsibility should not be understated. Of course, a more adequate attitude toward pollution would emanate from the realization that the earth deserves to be respected for its own sake as well as for generations yet unborn.

Industrial Response to Dwindling Supplies of Energy and Raw Materials

The rise of the industrial society with its corresponding effects on the environment has happened in a very short period of time. As Jim MacNeill writes:

> Since 1900, the number of people inhabiting the earth has multiplied more than three times. The world economy has expanded 20 times. The consumption of fossil fuels has grown by a factor of 30, and industrial production has increased by a factor of 50; four-fifths of that increase has occurred since 1950. This scale of development has produced a world with new realities[12]

One of the realities which industry as well as the broader society needs to address immediately is the fact that the earth's store of raw materials and fossil fuels is being depleted at an alarming rate. The blunt fact that there are physical limits to our natural resources needs to be accepted and acted upon by the architects of commerce and industry.

Up until recently little attention was paid to the fact that the earth's resources exist in finite amounts. Furthermore, scant attention was given to the social and environmental implications of resource depletion. Because it is no longer possible to ignore the growing scarcity of natural resources, industry is beginning to engage in a process of adaptation to the new situation; it is also being challenged to face up to the broader social issues attendant to dwindling resources.

Industry's response to the scarcity of energy and raw materials has been to commit itself to an industrial ecosystem which will function in concert with natural ecosystems. According to Robert A. Frosch, a theoretical physicist, and Nicholas E. Gallopoulos, a chemical engineer, industry can adapt to today's reality by altering the way materials are used:

> Materials in an ideal industrial ecosystem are not depleted any more than those in a biological one are; a chunk of steel could potentially show up one year in a tin can, the next year in an automobile and 10 years later in the skeleton of a building. Manufacturing processes in an industrial ecosystem simply transform circulating stocks of materials from one shape to another; the circulating stock decreases when some material is unavoidably lost, and it increases to meet the needs of a growing population. Such recycling still requires the expenditure of energy and the unavoidable generation of wastes, but at much lower levels than are typical today.[13]

Some materials with industrial uses, such as manganese, and molybdenum, are in very short supply; others are in the process of being depleted. Minerals which are scarce are difficult to extract; for both reasons they are expensive. As a consequence they become less attractive to industry and industry reduces or eliminates their use. Since manufacturing processes continue, however, industry tends to adjust to new circumstances by making less of the mineral go further, by wasting little or none of it, by using substitutes for it, or by reuse through recycling. Industry also has the option of producing a very expensive product made with the scarce material, designed to last a long time and ultimately destined to be recycled.

Burning fossil fuels causes air pollution and contributes to global warming but industrial societies are energy dependent and have, up until now, seemed willing to accept the undesirable tradeoffs accompanying fossil fuel use. This state of affairs may soon be coming to an end, however, because the earth's store of fossil fuels is finite and, as we noted in Chapter 1, if current use patterns continue, it would be possible to exhaust them during the next century. A planned adaptation in response to the presently depleted supply of fossil fuels is suggested by Willis Harman, an advocate of energy-frugal societies:

- Reduce industrial consumption of energy by producing more durable, repairable goods (eliminating planned obsolescence), by designing for materials recycling, by altering production processes so that waste heat and materials from one process become inputs into another; change the product mix of the economy to include less energy-consumptive materials and services; disperse manufacturing to produce goods closer to raw material sources and to users; emphasize craftsmanship and aesthetic quality rather than quantity of goods; emphasize sophisticated but frugal technology (e.g., the integrated-circuit hand calculator).

- Reduce personal energy requirements by dispersing population to reduce transportation needs from residence to place of work, by increasing dependence on communication instead of transportation (utilizing electronic communications and miniaturized information processing systems), by curbing consumption of energy-intensive goods and services, and by stimulating community-based recreation instead of long-distance travel.

- Redesign communities to be more self-sufficient and better suited to the environment and ecology, while using sophisticated technology to support highly civilized living conditions, not primitive privation (e.g., by using local solar heating, . . . by reducing requirements for transportation).[14]

The innovative genius of United States industry should be directed to the development of new sources of energy. The invention of substitutes for fuelwood which could be used in developing countries would represent a remarkable breakthrough. By focusing research efforts on solar energy, wind power, minihydroturbines, the recycling of waste biomass and the deployment of biomass digestors for making gas and liquid fuel,[15] industry could develop new energy sources to replace fossil fuels. Some industrialized countries rely heavily on nuclear energy. For example, France generates approximately 90% of its electrical power needs by nuclear means. Although there is at present great reluctance to adopt nuclear energy in the United States because of the lack of a clearly safe method for disposal of spent nuclear fuel, there are many advocates of nuclear energy as an acceptable solution to the fossil fuel shortage.

While industry may be able to successfully adapt to dwindling supplies of raw materials and fossil fuels, the harms to the environment already suffered as a result of clearcutting tropical forests in Third World countries are incalculable. Therefore, there should be no further leveling of rainforests. Regardless of who might profit from the sale of timber or the short-lived conversion of rainforest acreage to grazing or farmland, no industrial or social reason can be proposed which would justify the long-term harms to indigenous populations and to the environment. It is unclear what steps United States industry should take to begin to repair the damage which has already been done, but it is apparent that this issue should be addressed with the utmost earnestness.

During the past two decades, the poorer countries of the developing world have experienced a massive depletion of (their tropical forests). Just 40 years ago Ethiopia, for example, had a 30 percent forest cover; 12 years ago it was down to 4 percent, and today it may be 1 percent. Until this century India's forests covered more than half of the country. Today they are down to 14 percent and are going fast. In the tropics, 10 trees are being cut for every one planted; in Africa, the ratio is 29 to one. Forest areas nearly equal to the size of the United Kingdom are disappearing every year. Brazil alone may be losing more than eight million hectares annually.[16]

The fact that petroleum and the trees of the rain forest were once abundant and are now scarce is obviously going to affect production in the United States and other industrialized countries as well, and it also raises other issues. Since the earth is the storehouse of minerals, fossil fuels and timber, why have these commodities brought a profit to only a limited number of the citizens of the earth? And, on what basis did those citizens who came to own these goods justify their ownership? The industrialized countries in which one-quarter of the world's population lives consume (and have consumed) 80% of the world's goods. How can the First World's conspicuous consumption be justified when people in the Second and Third Worlds routinely deal with scarcity and poverty? What are the ethical responsibilities of industrialized societies in regard to unequal distribution of the goods of the earth? Do industrialized societies owe any debt to the generations yet unborn who will inherit a polluted depleted planet? Adapting to scarcity, answering these hard questions while increasing global industrial production fivefold to tenfold over the next fifty years is the challenge which confronts industry:

> . . . the most urgent imperative of the next few decades is further rapid growth. A fivefold to tenfold increase in economic activity would be required over the next 50 years in order to meet the needs of a burgeoning world population as well as to begin to reduce mass poverty. . . .

> A fivefold to tenfold increase in economic activity translates into a colossal new burden on the ecosphere. Imagine what it means in terms of planetary investment in housing, transport, agriculture and industry.[17]

Technology and industry which have brought such improvements to the First World standard of living may be the only hope of the people of the Second and Third World. It is clearly an understatement to assert that the task confronting industrialized societies is torturously complex. To refuse to undertake the multifaceted task, however, would be to abandon the planet and all who call it home.

Agriculture Faces the Challenge of Sustainability

The challenge to agriculture is to find ways of feeding 10 billion people in the next century through methods that will boost food production without further degrading the environment. In order to achieve this global goal agriculture will have to deal efficiently with the problems it faces, abandon practices which cause harm to the environment and alter attitudes of complacency.

From the mid 1960s through the mid 1980s the Green Revolution occurred worldwide as a result of improved agricultural technology. The result was a 2.4% per year growth in food production.[18] This encouraging statistic may prompt naive optimism about the continuing ability of agricultural technology to respond to future food needs. This optimism, however, is easily tempered by predictions that cropland worldwide will decline by 7% in the 1990s as well as the knowledge that farmers have 24 billion tons fewer of topsoil each year to feed 86 million more people.[19]

Three of the biggest soil-related problems which agriculture faces are erosion, desertification and salinization. Wind, floods, poor cultivation practices, clearcutting forests and overgrazing pastureland cause soil erosion. Desertification refers to the abandonment of once fertile areas due to erosion; should greenhouse predictions come to pass future climatic changes may cause extensive desertification in middle and northern latitudes, what is now some of the world's richest farmland. Salinization is salt buildup in soil which damages the roots of growing plants. In addition to trying to prevent further erosion and salinization, farmers need to restore fertility to eroded lands which are still salvageable. Two nonsoil related tasks entail the obtaining of adequate water for irrigation and the maintenance of genetic diversity in plant species.

Crops need water in order to grow. The water presently in use for irrigation has, in general, been easy to obtain. As new acreage is farmed irrigation programs are likely to be costly because the water which is used will probably be difficult to obtain. In addition, fresh water is a finite resource, more available in some locales than in others, and may have to be used more sparingly and efficiently than has been the practice to date. In order to use water efficiently throughout the world, agricultural technology is investigating several promising approaches. One is a system of trickle irrigation through which water is applied continuously to roots so that salts do not build up. Bringing such technologies to the farm will be expensive but there is no question of desirability: the soil's fertility will be preserved and its continued productivity will be assured.

Agriculture depends on the availability of a wide range of plant species—genetic diversity—so that it can adapt new strains of crops which will be able to resist the crop diseases of the future. It is also important that agriculture develop new crops that have more food mass and less of leaf and root so as to meet the increased food needs of the world's growing population. While water for irrigation and genetic diversity for future adaptation are not goods that farmers throughout the world can sell at the market, like fertile soil they are goods which farmers cannot afford to ignore.

The continuing productivity of agriculture worldwide needs to be achieved in an environmentally responsible manner. Three environmental threats which are specific to agriculture involve the use of herbicides, pesticides and fertilizers. These substances—of relatively recent origin—have been known to infest ground water, poisoning it, and to commingle with the water in streams, rivers, lakes and oceans as a result of runoff. Herbicides and pesticides can also remain as a residue on fruits and vegetables and cause deleterious health consequences if ingested in sufficient quantity.

Fertilizers are applied to the soil to enrich it and enhance its productivity. Their efficacy has been apparent in terms of the bumper crops harvested during the past generation, especially by farmers in the United States. Fertilizers contain chemicals, however, and these can be harmful to humans, making both farmers and consumers wary of them. In a recent article Iowa farmers were surveyed concerning their attitudes about fertilizers. One farmer, Jack Nuendorff, voiced his personal concern: "Six of my neighbors died in the last two years (from cancer), including some young ones."[20] Even though scientists and environmental regulators have not conclusively linked farm chemicals to Iowa farmers' relatively high rates of some cancers, a grass roots movement has emerged in Iowa to replace chemical fertilizers with such interim crops as nitrogen-rich rye grass and alfalfa.

United States scientists working in agricultural research are also attempting to develop a plant that would "fix" nitrogen in the soil.

Pierre R. Crosson and Norman J. Rosenberg comment concerning this possibility:

> One of the main components of fertilizer is nitrogen. If plants other than legumes could be biologically engineered so as to "fix" nitrogen in the soil, the demand for fertilizer would be greatly reduced. A prime candidate for such a transformation is corn. The job will clearly require the resources of biotechnology, which make it possible to manipulate the genetic material of an organism directly. Biotechnology has already proved its worth in a number of applications related to animal production, and the engineering of a nitrogen-fixing corn is by no means out of reach. Indeed, Frederick Ausubel of the Harvard Medical School noted recently that "it is simply an extremely complex engineering job" that will almost certainly be accomplished within 50 years.[21]

The use of herbicides and pesticides to prevent weeds and insects from overrunning or destroying crops is giving rise to significant environmental concern. If these chemicals make their way into ground water or surface water they can cause partial or total contamination. Even though United States government authorities monitor residues on food and keep them within so-called acceptable risk levels, consumers are sceptical and fearful. This fear was recently responsible for a major change in agricultural practice: a 1988 grassroots movement opposing the spraying of apples with the chemical alar resulted in the discontinuance of its use. Food producers are also trying to respond to an increasing consumer demand for organically grown fruits and vegetables.

The problem faced by agriculture worldwide is a technological one: to keep pests from destroying crops and prevent excessive weed growth without using chemicals which have hazardous side effects. A strategy being studied to achieve this result is known as integrated pest management (IPM). Integrated pest management relies on limited use of chemical pest controls along with mechanical manipulation of the soil and biological innovations. The biological innovations include outsmarting insects by introducing new varieties of crops which mature before the insect population, arranging for an adequate supply of natural predators which consume pests, and burning all plant residues after the harvest so as to destroy insect larvae. Obviously, integrated pest management is a complex process which must be adapted from place to place and from crop to crop.

In conclusion, global agriculture faces a multitude of interrelated environmental issues. In view of the world's growing population there is an evident need to increase the earth's yield. This must be done at the same time that eroded and eroding soil are being restored to the extent possible. The water upon which agriculture is dependent exists in finite amounts; it needs to be conserved and, in some cases, will be difficult to obtain. Developing new crops tomorrow depends on preserving genetic diversity today. All of this needs to be accomplished while phasing out, limiting or strictly controlling the use of chemical fertilizers, herbicides and pesticides. This complex of considerations is rendered still more complicated by the fact that farmers earn their living by selling crops. Short term, no economic benefits accrue from land or water conservation or from research efforts directed toward developing new crops.

What Might Motivate Business and Agriculture to Exercise Environmental Responsibility?

We saw in the preceding chapters that people exercise environmental responsibility if they think that the species of nature have a "right" to exist or if their religious beliefs counsel a reverent attitude towards creation. Regardless of whether a sense of environmental responsibility proceeds from philosophical or religious assumptions this sense is freely incorporated into one's value system; it is not (nor can it be) imposed. Industry and agriculture are two of the most important economic institutions in contemporary society. They have adapted themselves to this pluralistic secular culture by remaining separate from establishments of religion as well as beliefs held on faith; they are also noncommittal in respect to the relative merits of various approaches to reaching ethical judgments. Industry and agriculture hold in common three things: self-interest, the need to make a profit in order to continue to exist and a pro-technology bias fueled by the needs to change and to stay competitive. Further growth in materialism and consumerism are essential for business because these attitudes create markets for products and contribute to economic growth. It would be unrealistic to expect industry and modern agriculture to endorse their dismantling in order to return to a simpler way of life which holds less hazards for the environment. If businesses are to act on behalf of the environment this will need to be accomplished through a deliberate choice to add environmental concern to other items already on the business agenda. One might say that the environmental laws on the books in the United States require business leaders to comply with them in order to avoid jail or fines; this, of course, is true. But I do not think that compliance with laws in itself is sufficient to bring about the restoration of the planet. In order for this to be accomplished business leaders would need to *really care* about the air, land and water, as well as about generations yet unborn.

At the present time leaders of business and agriculture are trying to formulate a rationale to support meaningful involvement in caring for the earth. There is no question that the personal moral and religious convictions which people hold motivate them whether they are at home, at church, in the boardroom or on the farm. By tacit agreement, however, these are considered to be private, not shared, values. There is a need, therefore, to discover and promulgate motivation which would respect industry and agribusiness as needed social and economic institutions while appealing to secular values which most people hold in common. Within the context of contemporary culture in the United States it might be possible to build commitment and consensus around the following ideas:

- If the environment becomes damaged beyond repair there will be no place in which to build, to grow or to sell products.

- In the interests of fairness industry and agriculture should leave their locales the same as they found them.

• Through ingenuity and innovation it is possible to put measures in place to safeguard the environment *and* turn a profit.

• Business and agricultural leaders as well as workers and farmers need to broaden their work-related ethics to include the norm: Do no harm to the environment.

• The needs of the present generation should not be our only concern; we also must take into consideration our responsibilities to future generations.

By incorporating ideas like these into their codes of ethics industry and agribusiness would be raising the overall consciousness about environmental responsibility and taking a critically important step towards halting environmental degradation. There is no question that in so doing they would be side-stepping such profound issues as the legitimacy of anthropocentrism and the intrinsic worth of nature, but it is unrealistic to expect industry and agribusiness to engage such theoretical matters, much less to resolve them. It is, however, realistic to ask whether industry and agriculture can be expected to adopt and implement a code of environmental responsibility on the basis of sincere interest in the earth or whether the articulation of such codes will be merely exercises in public relations. This question brings us to a review of the role government plays in respect to designing and enforcing environmental regulations.

Government's Interaction with Industry and Agriculture in the Interests of the Environment

There is a growing consensus among well-informed people that the earth's environment is endangered and that there is an urgent need to halt environmental degradation and, to the extent possible, to restore the earth's ecosystems. The roles of government in a democracy like the United States include passing laws and enforcing them. Ideally, legislators should be motivated by concern for the long-term common good of all citizens and the environment as well. In seeking to carry out this goal they should rise above pressures which are exerted by special interests. Unfortunately, the real life circumstances in which government operates are far from ideal. The vast majority of citizens are uninformed and/or apathetic about the workings of government in regard to environmental matters. Industry and agribusiness have many well-financed lobbies in place to influence legislation as well as political action committees to finance election campaigns of candidates sympathetic to their interests. One of the aims of these efforts is to prevent regulations—including those pertaining to the environment—which would cost business money from being passed. Environmental groups, on the other hand, also lobby—oftentimes against business interests and against politicians who are sympathetic to those interests. The result is the adversarial situation which now exists in which energy is diverted from addressing environmental concerns and instead is invested in contentious arguments.

In order to break the stalemate it will be necessary for the legislative and executive branches of government to take the lead in making an uncompromising commitment to the environment. Business leaders are unanimous in opposing the bureaucracy and costs which go with government regulations. In a nonregulated atmosphere, however, companies which do not have to invest money in environmental safeguards can sell their goods at a lower cost than companies which voluntarily inaugurate environmentally friendly practices; these latter companies will eventually go out of business because of their inability to stay competitive. In addition, the health of the environment will continue to deteriorate. It would seem that the only way to correct this situation is for government to pass uncompromising regulations and to see that they are enforced in spite of the problems that this will cause industry and agriculture.

The way the economy is structured today consumers pay part of the cost for products and society pays other costs. If I buy a package of batteries for three dollars, I get four D cell batteries, the state gets twenty-four cents in tax revenue, the retailer gets a profit and the manufacturer gets the remainder. The manufacturer receives enough to cover all the costs to the company of making the batteries plus a profit. I will use the batteries for as long as they work in my flashlights, then I will put them in the trash. The trash will eventually wind up in a landfill. Other batteries will also accumulate there. Over time the batteries will leak mercury, cadmium and nickel and these toxic substances may eventually seep into an aquifer. If this happens, people who live in the environs of the landfill may consume contaminated water until such time as the water is declared unfit for consumption. The water may also be used to provide irrigation for a farm in the area, leaving an unseen residue on the produce which is grown there. In all probability, some people who drink the water or consume the produce will be sickened. In addition, the community will have to spend money to seal the aquifer and to develop new sources of water. Who should pay the costs attendant to sickness and to acquiring new sources of water? What liability does the farmer bear? The fact that at the present time industry and agriculture do not pay the social costs connected with the goods they sell has only recently come to be recognized. The role which government should play in determining who is responsible for what damages and collecting appropriate penalties is only beginning to be considered. In the absence of other institutions comparable in authority and jurisdiction to government, in all likelihood it is a responsibility which government will someday have to assume. If industry and agriculture realize that long-term they may be required by government to pay the social costs attendant to environmental damage caused by their products, this may motivate them to be more cautious and innovative in the design process so as to lessen or eliminate environmental harm caused by their products.

The environmental crisis is an enormously complex problem consisting of countless specific issues. In order for government to act effectively it needs to prioritize issues and design a comprehensive program to deal effectively with the current situation. In this regard J. Michael McCloskey, Chairperson of the Sierra Club, is reported as counseling:

> . . . focusing too much attention on "minor issues" such as landfills and questions of paper versus plastic bags. "We need to appreciate a hierarchy of values in this field and focus our best efforts on the momentous issues of the day."

> . . . They include ozone depletion, the greenhouse effect, the spraying of toxics into the air and environment, trade in

endangered species, tropical forest management and turning the trends around on pollution.[22]

Federal and state governments have passed many laws relating to the environment. At the federal level three agencies with environmentally relevant functions are the U.S. Food and Drug Administration, the Occupational Safety and Health Administration and the Environmental Protection Agency. The FDA, established after passage of the Food and Drug Act of 1906, has for its mission the protection of the public from impure and unsafe foods, drugs, cosmetics and other potential hazards. An office of the FDA, the National Center for Toxicological Research, conducts research programs to study the biological effects of potentially toxic chemicals found in the environment. The research Center is especially interested in the health effects on people of long term exposure to low level chemical toxicants such as those found in the air or as residues on farm products and as contained in contaminated meat and fish. Research at the Center is carried out on animals; scientists extrapolate using animal data, projecting possible or probable consequences for humans.

The Occupational Safety and Health Administration was established in 1970 to develop workplace safety and health standards. In this regard OSHA develops and issues regulations, conducts investigations and inspections to monitor compliance with its standards, and issues citations for noncompliance with these standards. OSHA is, therefore, the government agency charged with overseeing the health and safety of people who work with hazardous chemicals and designing safeguards to protect them from injury in the workplace.

The Environmental Protection Agency was established in 1970 to be an independent agency devoted to controlling and abating pollution in the areas of air, water, solid waste, pesticides, radiation and toxic substances. Its mandate is to forge a coordinated attack on environmental pollution in cooperation with state and local governments. The purpose of the EPA is to serve as the public's advocate for a livable environment. The Superfund program, designed to clean up hazardous waste dump sites, under terms of CERCLA (the Comprehensive Environmental Response,

Compensation and Liability Act of 1980) is conducted under the auspices of the EPA. In this regard, parties responsible for past dumping of hazardous wastes are tracked down and required to clean up dump sites or pay the government to carry out the clean up. To date 1,200 sites have been placed on the Superfund National Priorities List to be cleaned up.

Two major laws dealing with environmental protection were passed in 1970 and 1972, have been amended as necessary, and are in force today.

• The Clean Air Act of 1970 was enacted in order to "protect and enhance the nation's air resources so as to promote the public health," "to achieve the prevention and control of air pollution," and to assist the state in establishing programs with these ends in view.[23] At this writing both houses of Congress have passed legislation which would revise and expand the Clean Air Act for the first time in 13 years. The bills under consideration vary considerably in their prescriptions for acid rain, toxic pollutants, automobile emissions and urban smog.

• The Clean Water Act of 1972 was enacted to clean up surface water in the United States. The CWA prohibits the discharge of any pollutant into a navigable waterway unless that discharge is allowed by a National Pollution Discharge Elimination Systems (NPDES) permit. Discharge limits are set for specific pollutants on an industry-by-industry basis, and are incorporated into a NPDES permit for "direct discharges" into conduits leading to surface waters, or into pretreatment standards for industries that discharge to local publicly-owned treatment works. The act uses a technology-based system for setting standards.

How effective has the government been in regulating agriculture and business? Consider the answer given by William K. Reilly, Administrator of the EPA in 1989, and evaluate it in relation to your own perception of the state of the environment:

Twenty years ago, the Cuyahoga River in Cleveland occasionally would catch on fire. We would hear daily that many of our lakes and waterways were on the verge of dying from eutrophication due to discharge of phosphates and other pollutants. Our eyes and throats burned from auto exhaust and emissions from industrial plants. Earth Day (1970) was a chance for citizens to say, "Enough." As a society, we demanded that our government take action to protect us and future generations from the dangers of environmental pollution. The Congress and the President responded with the creation of the Environmental Protection Agency and the swift passage of two landmark pieces of legislation—the Clean Air Act Amendments of 1970 and the Clean Water Act of 1972. In the years since then, many other environmental statutes have been passed, and we have made great strides in abating pollution. EPA and the States have developed plans to abate pollution, issued permits governing industrial discharges, and taken enforcement actions to compel compliance with environmental laws.[24]

Conclusion

The human species has always altered the environment. Since the Industrial Revolution, however, the extent to which humans have altered the planet has been immense. Widespread environmental degradation has been the result. As we look to the future we need to decide what to do about restoring eroded lands, polluted air and waters as well as how to interpret and deal with the effects of ozone depletion and climate changes. These are massive issues, complex and global, to which modern industrial and agricultural practices contribute in no small measure. There is an urgent need for industry and agriculture to stop doing things which harm the environment and to put environmentally friendly practices in place. Given this real world we all inhabit—with its admixture of the noble and nefarious—there is scant reason to believe that an ethos of environmental responsibility will emerge spontaneously or painlessly. The role of government is, therefore, crucial in regulating industry and agriculture and its integrity needs to be beyond question so that the common good will be the overarching concern.

Case Study:

This case study is based on four news accounts which appeared in *The New York Times* between April and July, 1990.[25]

There are an estimated 3,000 pairs of spotted owls in the United States; their habitats are the forests of Northern California, Oregon and Washington. Three groups are enmeshed in a conflict concerning logging in the forests and the preservation of the owls: environmentalists, the timber industry and government.

The environmentalists contend that the sale of federally owned forests to timber companies has imperiled endangered species in the past and threatens the spotted owl today. Environmental groups want forests left intact for many ecological reasons in addition to the preservation of endangered species and natural habitats. They consider protection of the spotted owl under the provisions of the Endangered Species Act the best legal weapon available to them to save the forests. Environmentalists respond to economic arguments by timber industry spokespersons to continue cutting in the forests by saying that projected job loss figures are inflated. Leaders of the environmental movement say that there is no middle ground available to government through which the government could protect some forest land on behalf of the spotted owl and endorse the sale of other land to the timber interests. They maintain that if George Bush's administration tries to put a compromise in place no one will be satisfied and a dangerous precedent will be set. Environmental groups say that they will bring lawsuits to halt logging if any steps are taken by government to undermine the protected status due to the spotted owl.

Chris West of the Northwest Forestry Association said on June 23, 1990, "We don't believe the owl is threatened, we think the environmentalists are trying to put us out of business." The timber industry's main interest is in preserving its economic viability. If forests are declared off-limits to loggers in order to protect the spotted owl, there would be a 25% reduction in the amount of timber which is cut. Such a reduction would result in the near term loss of 10,000 jobs, with as many as 28,000 jobs disappearing within ten years. On average, loggers make $8.00 to $13.00 per hour; by converting to jobs in the service sector their earnings would be cut in half. Loggers give evidence of seeing themselves as victims of an elected government which could take their livelihood from them. They are challenging the government which is threatening to take their jobs away to care for them in such an eventuality. They are also protesting the stress which accompanies the uncertainty and precariousness of their situation.

After a comprehensive study carried out by scientists for the Fish and Wildlife Service the spotted owl was declared an endangered species on June 23, 1990, and a recommendation was made that 2.5 million acres of forest in the Pacific Northwest be declared off-limits to logging. Under the terms of the Endangered Species Act there is no doubt that the spotted owl should now be the subject of government protection. A federal order could keep loggers from cutting and it seems unlikely that, if such an order is forthcoming, the government would render any economic assistance to those who become unemployed. The government, however, is uncomfortable with a black and white resolution of the situation. It is, therefore, seeking to put a compromise in place. Some of the avenues being explored are encouraging the sale of privately owned lands and designing a strategy whereby much less than 2.5 million acres are reserved for the preservation of the spotted owl. To this end a new study group was appointed on June 21, 1990, and was instructed to submit its report to the president by September 1, 1990. There is speculation that this group may be able to come up with a plan to protect the spotted owl which will cost only 1,000 jobs. Discussion is also ongoing about the possibility of revising the Endangered Species Act so that a species would not have to be afforded anything close to absolute protection should severe economic disruption occur. The proper way to interpret the Endangered Species Act is also being reviewed to determine how much, if any, leeway the act allows.

- In order to formulate one's opinion on this case, why would it be necessary to determine whether one's approach to nature is anthropocentric or egalitarian?

- Which is more important, the income of a logger or the spotted owl? Why?

- What steps do environmentalists need to take in order to strengthen their case?

• What are the long term ramifications of declaring the habitat of the spotted owl off-limits to loggers? What are the short term ramifications? Can people with different interests be expected to come up with conflicting answers to these questions? Why?

• What should the government do in respect to the Endangered Species Act and the spotted owl? Why? Would you characterize your response to this question as idealistic, realistic, pragmatic—or by some other term? Why?

Questions for Discussion

1. If you were the CEO of an industrial corporation whose operations had obvious environmental impact, and you were sincerely committed to ethical leadership, describe the safeguards you would put in place to make certain that your firm would not foul the environment.

2. If you were the employee of a manufacturing firm or a farmer who worked for a large agricultural concern, what type of incentives and assurances on the part of management would prompt you to exercise care for the environment? How inclined would you be to take initiatives on behalf of the environment if management did not seem to be concerned? How would you feel in your action or complacency if you were employed by a firm which was hostile or indifferent to the care of the environment?

3. State five steps which industry can take to reduce waste and reduce/eliminate pollution. How much waste and pollution are acceptable? State the criteria which should be used to determine an acceptable level of pollution.

4. If a commodity such as aluminum or timber is called a "raw material," what assumptions are implicit in the act of naming it? How do you think past and present generations have come to think of raw materials as being in or on the earth for their use? What rights do future generations have in respect to the raw materials which are being depleted today?

5. Outline the procedure you would follow to determine if you or your present/future children were at risk from fertilizers, herbicides and pesticides. What degree of risk should an adult be willing to take? An infant? A young child? What would cause you to decide that a risk was too great for you or your child?

6. What steps does agriculture have to take in order to produce enough food to meet the nutritional requirements of the world's growing population? Do you think agriculture is going to be able to meet this challenge? Why or why not?

7. Compare the moral motivations for environmental responsibility contained in Chapter 2 and the religious motivations described in Chapter 3 with those suggested as appropriate for business and agriculture in this chapter. Are there areas of convergence? What ideas do you find persuasive, and why?

8. What steps should government take to reverse environmental degradation? Are there any concessions government should agree/refuse to make in order to put effective controls in place? Be specific in listing these concessions.

9. What laws have been passed and agencies established to protect the environment in the United States? What additional laws, agencies and/or policies need to be put in effect?

Debate

Resolved: In the interests of stockholders, employees and consumers, business should intervene in the political arena for the purpose of defeating and weakening environmental regulations.

For Further Reading

Herman E. Daly and John B. Cobb, Jr., *For the Common Good: Redirecting the Economy toward Community, the Environment, and a Sustainable Future*, (Boston: Beacon Press, 1989).

Manuel G. Velasquez, *Business Ethics*, (Second Edition), (New Jersey: Prentice Hall, 1988), Chapter 5, Ethics and the Environment.

Scientific American, 261:3, September, 1989, pp. 118-174.

Glossary

CEO: Chief Executive Officer.

Pragmatism: A philosophy which is less interested in abstract theory than in practical strategies which will achieve a desired goal. Policy-makers in agriculture, business and government tend, for the most part, to be pragmatists.

End Notes

1. Kenneth E. Goodpaster and Norman Bowie, "Corporate Conscience, Money and Motorcars," *Business Ethics Report*, 1989, p. 4.

2. p. 4.

3. Manuel G. Velasquez, "Ethics and the Environment," in *Business Ethics* (New Jersey: Prentice Hall, 1988), p. 246.

4. "U.S. to Test New Atomic Waste Disposal Plan," *The New York Times*, July 31, 1990, p. A16.

5. George Sammet, Jr. and William J. Schwalm, "Corporate Strategies for Environmental Protection," in *Business Ethics Report*, p. 9.

6. Richard W. Stevenson, "United Parcel to Alter Its Trucks in Los Angeles to Create Less Smog," *The New York Times*, July 11, 1990, p. B6.

7. Matthew L. Wald, "Designing Tankers to Minimize Oil Spills," *The New York Times*, June 17, 1990, p. 5. Wald cites the American Petroleum Institute as the source for the quoted material.

8. John Holusha, "DuPont to Construct Plants for Ozone-Safe Refrigerant," *The New York Times*, June 23, 1990, p. 31.

9. p. 32.

10. Robert A. Frosch and Nicholas E. Gallopoulos, "Strategies for Manufacturing," *Scientific American*, 261:3, September, 1989, p. 152.

11. p. 150.

12. Jim MacNeill, "Strategies for Sustainable Economic Development," *Scientific American*, p. 155.

13. Frosch and Gallopoulos, p. 146.

14. Willis W. Harman, *An Incomplete Guide to the Future*, (San Francisco: San Francisco Book Company, 1976), p. 47.

15. MacNeill, p. 162.

16. p. 157.

17. p. 156.

18. Pierre R. Crosson and Norman J. Rosenberg, "Strategies for Agriculture," *Scientific American*, p. 132.

19. Matthew L. Wald, "Guarding Environment: A World of Challenges," *The New York Times*, April 22, 1990, p. 25.

20. Knight-Ridder News Service, "Concerned with Costs, Health, Farmers Rethink Chemical Use," *The Record*, June 5, 1990, p. B8.

21. Crosson and Rosenberg, p. 132.

22. J. Michael McCloskey, "Customers as Environmentalists," *Business Ethics Report*, p. 11.

23. Pub. L. 90-148, 2, 81 Stat. 485.

24. William K. Reilly, Letter, *EPA Enforcement Accomplishments Report: FY 1989* (Washington, D.C.: U-S-EPA, 1990), p. 1.

25. Timothy Egan, "10,000 Are Expected to Lose Jobs to Spotted Owl," April 28, 1990, p. 8; Timothy Egan, "U.S. Declares Owl Threatened by Heavy Logging," June 23, 1990, p. 1; Timothy Egan, "Softening Stand on Spotted Owl, Administration Delays Protection," June 27, 1990; Philip Shabecoff, "In Thicket of Environmental Policy, Bush Uses Balance as His Compass," July 1, 1990, p. 20; all in *The New York Times*.

Chapter Five

The Individual and Commitment to the Common Good

Introduction

There is no question that many different factors impact on the environment. People who assume that trees and wildlife have rights will conduct themselves differently from people who assume that trees and wildlife exist for human use. People who believe that nature belongs to God or is sacred will be much more restrained in their conduct towards nature than people who think that God has no involvement in nature. And people who include environmental costs when making economic calculations are much more likely to take measures designed to reduce pollution and waste and to lessen reliance on nonrenewable natural resources than people who do not. As we have seen thus far in this book, underlying presuppositions and beliefs translate into generalizable attitudes which are broadly characteristic of the way a society views the environment; it is these attitudes which in large measure dictate the way in which people approach the environment.

The purpose of this chapter is to focus on the autonomous individual, the reflective person who is willing to take the time to become informed, make independent decisions, and take steps to enhance the environment. Rachel Carson, born in 1907, recipient of a Master's Degree in biology, employee of the United States Bureau of Fisheries, and author in 1962 of *A Silent Spring,* will forever be remembered for her love of nature. In her most famous work Rachel Carson warned that a silent spring in which no birds would sing was a distinct possibility which could result from the transmittal of insecticide poisoning throughout the food chain. Millions of individuals, heeding Carson's warnings, began to be concerned about tampering with the web of life. Some of these people who shared Carson's love of nature and fear for its well-being became activists in the environmental movement. Like Rachel Carson they have made, and are making, a difference. So, too, can every individual who resolves so to do.

Overcoming Negativism

If individuals are to become personally committed to the well-being of the earth, they will need to overcome pervasive tendencies to negativism. Given the scope of environmental degradation and the inclination to think that the cumulative problems are insurmountable, counteracting negative attitudes is the first step in restoring the environment.

One way of promoting negativism is by staying uninformed. Whether or not one states explicitly, "I don't want to know," it is simple enough to remain in the dark. By avoiding media coverage of environmental issues and being too busy to attend education sessions we can deny the existence of complex environmental problems which do not cause direct harm to us. Calling apathy a national plague, a *New York Times* report on two studies of young people's attitudes was especially concerned about the indifference of people aged 20 to 29 in regard to matters of public interest. Describing young people as not wanting to know about issues of concern to the larger world, the author Michael Oreskes speculated that today's young people are rebelling against rebellion; they have "become cynical without going through the activism and disappointment that produced that cynicism"[1] for previous generations. While shielding ourselves from matters that are unpleasant or seem overwhelming is a tendency common to people of all ages, the prevalence of this attitude among people under thirty is particularly worrisome because the formulation of public policy will soon be in their hands.

As problematic as it is to adopt an "I don't want to know" attitude, it is worse to posit an attitude of "I don't care." If we are not too troubled by the effects of environmental degradation and the way things are in our backyard is pretty much to our liking, it might be tempting to forgo altruistic concerns about other humans and nature and be content about the quality of the existence which we enjoy. Of course, in so doing we would be denying the inexorable inroads of pollution everywhere, even in our backyards, and we would be excusing ourselves from involvement in a movement which holds promise of benefit for ourselves and our children as well as for people throughout the world.

Given the scope of environmental degradation it can be difficult for well-intentioned people to believe that their efforts can make a difference. It is easy to deprecate the value of one individual's potential for making an impact and to think "I don't count; there is nothing I can do to make a difference." If in spite of a generally benevolent attitude towards nature we give in to such a defeatist attitude, there is no doubt that the environment will continue to be destroyed. In addition, we will be overlooking the positive accomplishments which can be brought about through simple lifestyle changes which anyone can adopt with a minimum of inconvenience.

One of the hardest negative attitudes to combat is the one which suggests "Let George or Georgette do it." Passing the buck because one is too busy, too weary, or just not up to the challenge is an old and familiar ploy. It is also an evasion of personal responsibility and a certain way to insure that the significant work of restoring the earth's ecosystems is postponed indefinitely.

Cultivating indifference toward environmental issues because problems such as ozone depletion and global warming will likely reach the critical phase only after one's demise is another way for people to evade taking personal interest in the environment. They manage to ignore the pollution and acid rain which are already degrading the environment while refusing to be concerned about future catastrophes. By so doing, short-sighted people keep themselves on an even keel today and do not worry about tomorrow. They absolve themselves of responsibility for the world all our children will inherit. Even though they have the ability to keep themselves from being weighed down by environmental issues, it is difficult to imagine how personal serenity can coexist with such selfishness.

If negative attitudes expressive of disinterest, fatalism and selfishness characterize the response of many individuals toward the environmental crisis, these sentiments are certainly capable of undermining attempts to heal the earth. It is, therefore, of the utmost importance that negative attitudes be confronted and counteracted in order that society commit itself to acting responsibly on behalf of the environment. One way to accomplish this goal is by expanding our horizon so that we no longer see humans solely as isolated, autonomous individuals but we also understand and affirm our interconnectedness as well as our roles in relation to the common good.

Becoming Committed to the Common Good

It would be an oversimplification to divide society into two parts: people who are out for themselves and people who have the common good at heart. The 250 million people who live in the United States defy such facile categorization. This does not mean, however, that the highly credible social analysis of Robert Bellah and others[2] is inaccurate or unconvincing. On the contrary, it is quite apparent that our society encourages and supports the satisfaction of autonomous individuals over and above concern for the common good. It is also obvious that many of us have internalized a self-centered, me-first value system.

Thinking of persons as completely autonomous and encouraging the pursuit of personal satisfaction leads to understanding individuals as existing for themselves and driven by the need for self-gratification. Individual rights count for much more than personal responsibilities and it is primarily in the interest of securing these rights that efforts are expended. The sense that there is one human family, one web of life, one global village receives only token recognition, and the ties that bind this present generation to generations past and future tend to be disregarded. To those who emphasize individual autonomy and self-satisfaction, the marketplace, other individuals and nature are approached in order to obtain what one wants or needs. Thus, a calculating crassness is encountered more frequently than a respectful reverence towards people and nature. Although there is abundant evidence that individualism is the dominant strand in contemporary culture, the question as to its appropriateness should not go unchallenged.

In my opinion we manifest a profound confusion about what it means to be human when we live our lives without honoring our interconnections and interdependencies. Human persons are unique and distinctive because of the genetic and cultural endowment received from their forebears. We are social by nature and we need companionship. We turn to others to celebrate our joys with us and to help us bear our burdens. These others are most frequently family members, friends, neighbors or colleagues but they might even be strangers. The support and practical advice proffered by people initially encountered as strangers in self-help groups make it possible to manage the most difficult aspects of our lives. When we join church communities, political parties, civic associations, recreational leagues and other groups we express and sustain our personal interests through involvement with like-minded people. To isolate oneself or dismiss the importance of handing on one's values, belongings *and habitat* to one's posterity is to miss what it means to be a person in community or a human being. There is a critical need for us to move beyond thinking of ourselves in solely individualistic terms and to claim our identity as individuals with many profound connections. Should society reinstate interdependence and connectedness as among the most important of human attributes this would be a welcome corrective; it would also signal a major change of direction because awareness of community is the essential prerequisite for establishing a sense of commitment to the common good. If individuals knew themselves to be inextricably bound up with others, the well-being of the other would take on a new importance. In addition, acknowledging the necessity of working for the common good would lead to exercising concern for the environment, if not for its own sake, then on account of the way people can be positively or negatively affected by it.

What is the "common good"? The common good refers to the prosperity and well-being of a tribe, a nation, a federation, a religious or ethnic group, or all people everywhere. Acting on behalf of the common good means to undertake measures or enact policies which will be of unmistakable benefit to all. Eliminating pollution, universal dismantling of the weapons of war or insuring an adequate food supply for everyone on earth would be actions promotive of the common good. The common good of all would be achieved if people enjoyed political, social and religious freedom, societal structures were just, there was economic stability, violence and lawlessness were nonexistent, the needs of the widow, the orphan, the sick and the handicapped were met, educational and vocational opportunities were offered to all young people and the elderly held a place of esteem in society. The common good, as just portrayed, is an ideal state, a state which will never be perfectly attained, but one which people are inclined to seek provided that they are not self-absorbed and indifferent to others.

Pursuit of the common good is motivated by the insight that the common good is a noble, worthy goal, the belief that all persons have inherent dignity and rights which ought to be safeguarded, and the conviction that it makes sense to act with the welfare of others in mind and it is foolish to persist in the obsessive pursuit of self-gratification. If there were a shift in the way we relate to ourselves and others so that interest in the common good becomes a primary concern, how might this attitudinal change affect the environment? If "we the people" were committed to the common good over the long haul, we would find it mandatory to take steps to halt environmental degradation. Bolstered by the knowledge that indigenous peoples suffer more than anyone else when tropical forests are clearcut and pollution jeopardizes everyone's health—now and in the future—we could not keep silent as rainforests are laid bare and smokestacks belch. In addition, knowing that it is unfair for one group to prosper through actions which are environmentally irresponsible, such as using toxic fertilizers to increase agricultural production in the short term, would prompt an irate outcry.

The particular conceptualization of the common good which is solely or primarily concerned with the members of the human family is anthropocentric; it is also a vast improvement over the self-centered approach which pays no heed to the needs of other people. If one's approach to the common good is broader and more inclusive so that it encompasses all species, one's agenda will be different. The survival, well-being and flourishing of all living species would be assessed as desirable in itself, not merely because of what they contribute to humans. In both anthropocentric and egalitarian approaches to the common good there would be a willingness to make personal sacrifices and lifestyle adjustments for the benefit of others. If the reflective autonomous individual to whom we referred at the beginning of this chapter comprehends the importance of working towards the common good and understands the inherent contradiction in conceiving of the human person as isolated from other persons and nature, then that person would be prepared to take concrete initiatives in the exercise of environmental responsibility.

Exercising Care and Concern for the Environment

Individuals who care about other people and about the earth can adopt lifestyle changes which will help to heal the earth. In addition to making lifestyle changes they can also make an impact by becoming advocates for the environment and by keeping themselves informed about issues of consequence to the environment. Let us consider twenty-five lifestyle changes which will benefit the earth and all the life forms to which it is home.

Lifestyle Changes

1. Modify consumerist inclinations. Although the economy of the United States is structured around the marketplace and advertising tries to seduce us to buy a myriad of products, the well-being of the earth requires that we content ourselves with fewer possessions, more modest abodes and less dependence on material things. If, in our resolve to walk lightly on the earth, we

buy and use less, economic structures will unfailingly adapt to changing patterns.

2. Drive less, use public transportation or car pool. Since automobiles contribute to air pollution and global warming we need to curtail their use. Getting in the habit of walking or biking short distances instead of driving would be a step in the right direction.

3. Buy major appliances which have high energy efficiency ratings and buy cars which have the best gas mileage. In this way we will be cutting down on the pollution caused by fossil fuels and conserving energy.

4. Don't tamper with auto emission controls and keep cars tuned up so as to minimize tailpipe pollution.

5. Have a home energy audit conducted by a representative of your heating utility. To keep heat from escaping, install insulation and storm windows and apply caulk around windows and doors. Have the furnace serviced every two years so that it operates as efficiently as possible. Turn the temperature down a few degrees, and wear a sweater to keep warm.

6. Use less hot water at the basin and in the shower. By installing low flow faucet heads the amount of water will be permanently reduced.

7. Install a clothes line and let the sun and wind dry your laundry. Only use a clothes dryer in inclement weather.

8. Turn off lights when not in use. Since lighting uses one-fifth of all energy, switching to compact fluorescent bulbs which use seventy-five percent less energy than standard light bulbs can make a substantial difference.

9. Wait until the dishwasher and washing machine are full before running them. Whenever possible wash laundry with cold water.

10. Use solar-powered flashlights and calculators. Consider installing passive solar heating and solar water heaters.

11. Plant trees so as to lower carbon dioxide in the atmosphere. The shade from trees can cool homes and reduce the need for air conditioning.

12. Have air conditioners and refrigerators serviced by contractors who recycle CFCs rather than discharging them so as to prevent further damage to the ozone layer.

13. Avoid styrofoam. It is not biodegradable and CFCs are used in its manufacture. Keeping a coffee mug at work and having one in the car will help do away with the need for styrofoam.

14. Precycle. Buy large sizes and goods packaged in reusable containers. Keep harmful materials from entering the waste stream by rejecting them at their source.

15. Recycle newspapers, cardboard, glass, metals and plastics. Recycling saves trees, other natural resources, money and energy.

16. Take a cloth or string tote bag on shopping trips or bring used paper grocery bags back to the supermarket; they can be used again and again. Some supermarket chains are offering a small cash incentive of five cents a bag for customers who reuse paper bags.

17. Don't use paper diapers. Plastic linings don't disintegrate for hundreds of years and soft wood pulp is used to make the paper part. In addition, three million tons of feces and urine from paper diapers end up in landfills each year posing a danger to groundwater.

18. Start composting. Food scraps and garden clippings can easily be turned into compost and used as organic fertilizer.

19. Eat low on the food chain—more fruits, vegetables and grains. In this way there will be less domestic demand for meat and more food will be available worldwide.

20. Buy locally grown food whenever possible so as to discourage long distance transport.

21. Use rechargeable batteries because they last much longer than alkaline batteries. Although rechargeable batteries contain

cadmium they have the advantage of not containing mercury, a very hazardous substance present in alkaline batteries.

22. Snip six-pack plastic rings before you dispose of them so that if they wind up in a body of water they will not choke fish.

23. Don't use detergents with a phosphate content of more than 0.5% because phosphates often wind up in lakes and streams where they cause algae blooms which destroy marine life.

24. Don't use pesticides in the house or garden. Pesticides contain toxic chemicals which can harm much more than the insects for which they are intended. Homemade remedies such as washing surfaces with a solution of vinegar and water or sprinkling bone meal, chili powder or lemon juice at points of entry can protect against infestation without hazardous side effects.

25. Don't use oil-based paints, thinners, solvents, stains or finishes because they contain toxic ingredients and hazardous liquid wastes are generated during their manufacture. Disposal of unused portions inevitably leads to contamination of land, water or air.

Becoming Committed to Advocacy

Lifestyle changes need to be coupled with a commitment to advocacy. Here are ten ways in which we can become spokespersons for the earth.

1. Discuss environmental issues with family and friends around the dinner table. Begin at home to raise environmental consciousness.

2. Promote energy efficiency at the workplace and suggest the formulation of a corporate policy of environmental responsibility.

3. Lobby for media coverage of environmental news. Make the point that attending to ecology on Earth Day is not enough.

4. Write letters to the editor to bring environmental concerns to light.

5. Encourage churches, libraries, community groups and businesses to sponsor forums on environmental issues.

6. Suggest that interdisciplinary courses on the environment be included in grade school, high school and college curricula.

7. Phone or write to legislative and executive leaders in order to urge measures aimed at environmental preservation and/or restoration.

8. Visit local newspapers, schools and businesses and ask them to switch to recycled paper and to take other environmentally friendly initiatives.

9. Speak out against products which contain toxic ingredients such as styrofoam, pesticides, oil-based paints and detergents containing phosphates.

10. Encourage the development of so-called "green products" such as paper towels made from recycled paper by requesting that markets stock them.

In order to adopt an environmentally responsible lifestyle and to be well informed advocates for the earth we need to keep up-to-date with relevant developments. It is also imperative that we secure the support and affirmation which are necessary to sustain our commitment. For these reasons it would be a very good idea to join one or more groups which are devoted to environmental issues. A representative list follows.

Audubon Society
950 Third Ave.
New York, NY 10022

Environmental Action Foundation
1525 New Hampshire Ave., NW
Washington, DC 20036

Environmental Policy Institute
218 D St., SE
Washington, DC 20003

Friends of the Earth
530 Seventh St., SE
Washington, DC 20003

Greenpeace
1436 U St., NW
Washington, DC 20009

National Parks & Conservation Association
1015 31st St., NW
Washington, DC 20007

National Wildlife Federation
1412 16th St., NW
Washington, DC 20036

Sierra Club
730 Polk St.
San Francisco, CA 94109

United Nations Environmental Programme
DC 2 - 0803 United Nations
New York, NY 10017

World Wildlife Fund/Conservation Foundation
1250 24th St., NW
Washington, DC 20037

Conclusion

Parents who have cradled their newborn children in their arms speak of the awesome feelings of inadequacy and responsibility which accompany this experience. In almost every case the total dependence of infants on their parents brings out the best in fathers and mothers, and families prosper. In those terribly tragic cases in which parents neglect or abuse their babies, the babies' only recourse is to cry or to withdraw.

To picture the earth as cradled in human hands is to envision the earth's ecosystems as fragile, vulnerable and dependent on human care. Recognizing the human task of protecting and preserving the earth may engender feelings similar to those of parents of newborns. At this stage in the evolution of life the earth is cradled in human hands; by human deeds it can be replenished as the abundant source of life. Or through human malice and indifference it can continue to deteriorate, becoming in time the harbinger of death. The choice is ours. The time is now.

Case Study

When she was a junior Melissa decided to start a chapter of Students for Environmental Action at her high school. When she told her parents about her idea they said that in general they approved but they had reservations because taking on such a big commitment would probably have an adverse effect on her grades and rank in class. Melissa's friends offered her little encouragement. One or two thought that environmental concern was overstated, others stereotyped environmental advocates as nonconformists who feel compelled to become vegetarians. Most of Melissa's friends, good students like her, said that the reason they were diligent and studious was because they wanted to earn the credentials which would allow them to succeed within the system; they had no intention of challenging it.

A few of the students to whom Melissa spoke expressed guarded interest. They asked to be kept informed about what she intended to do and said that they were interested in observing how her involvement would be played out. In spite of the lack of encouragement, Melissa decided to go ahead and establish an SEA branch. She networked with the leaders of SEA clubs at nearby high schools and learned the procedures to be followed in setting up a new branch. She dealt with all the paper work entailed in procuring administrative permission by herself and she advertised the first meeting by personally putting notices on every single bulletin board. To her surprise, eight students showed up for the first meeting, the two curious friends who said that they were interested in observing what she would do and six who were not part of her circle. The group concurred with Melissa that its first year should be devoted to self-education and they attended a number of programs with this end in view.

During her senior year Melissa was elected president of the SEA chapter which then numbered twelve members. The group organized three activities: the clean-up of a local wildlife area at which they were joined by members of the National Honor Society; a protest of wasted paper at a Board of Education meeting; and a boycott of the cafeteria because its director ignored their repeated requests to eliminate the use of styrofoam. Neither the Board of Education nor the cafeteria management changed their policies in response to SEA activism.

At the school's graduation ceremony Melissa received an award for her service to the community. Three of her new friends, the SEA slate of officers for the coming year, were there to applaud her.

- Would it be worth the price to see one's grades and class rank suffer in order to take on the responsibility of organizing a group to act on behalf of the environment?

- Are people who take initiatives on behalf of the environment abnormal or different?

- How can environmental activism become a part of the so-called "system"?

- Was Melissa stubborn, a visionary or foolish in taking so much start up responsibility on herself?

- Considering that neither the Board of Education nor the cafeteria management changed their policies in response to SEA requests, were the time and efforts Melissa and other members of the SEA expended worthwhile or not worthwhile? Why?

Questions for Discussion

1. What are you willing to do on behalf of the environment? Write a short essay in response to this question and do not overstate the extent to which you are willing to become involved.

2. Engage a friend, neighbor, colleague, teacher or fellow student in conversation about environmental problems. Challenge this person to do something to make a difference. How did he/she respond? Note excuses, level of interest, indications of activism, and prepare an oral or written report describing same.

3. Discuss why negative attitudes towards environmental issues bode ill for the future of the earth.

4. How do you see yourself: as an individual with personal goals and values pretty much uninvolved with others, or as a part of a larger group whose goals and values are at least as important as your own? Describe the connection of your self-perception to the attitude with which you approach nature.

5. State three reasons to move beyond individualism to commitment to the common good.

6. What is the common good? How would a societal commitment to the common good translate into action on behalf of the environment?

7. Twenty-five lifestyle changes are proposed in this chapter to help to heal the earth. Compose your own list of five additional items to supplement the compilation in this book.

8. Choose one of the ten ways suggested to express advocacy for the environment and develop an outline of how you would go about implementing it.

9. How do you feel about tackling environmental degradation? What help would you personally need if you were to get involved? What steps would you need to take to sustain your commitment?

Debate

Resolved: Since underlying presuppositions and beliefs translate into generalizable attitudes which are broadly characteristic of the way society views the environment, government, public education and the mainstream media in the United States ought to promote nonconsumerist values through subtle and forthright means.

For Further Reading

The Earth Works Group, *50 Simple Things You Can Do to Save the Earth* (Berkeley, CA: Earthworks Press, 1989).

Jeremy Rifkin, editor, *The Green Lifestyle Handbook* (New York: Henry Holt & Company, 1990).

End Notes

1. Michael Oreskes, "Profiles of Today's Youth: They Couldn't Care Less," *The New York Times*, June 28, 1990, pp. I,D21.

2. Cf., Robert Bellah, Richard Madsen, William M. Sullivan, Ann Swidler, and Steven M. Tipton, *Habits of the Heart* (New York: Harper & Row, 1985).

Books by Eileen P. Flynn

Human Fertilization in Vitro: A Catholic Moral Perspective, Lanham, MD, 1984.

My Country Right or Wrong? Selective Conscientious Objection in the Nuclear Age, Chicago, 1985.

AIDS: A Catholic Call for Compassion, Kansas City, 1985.

Teaching About AIDS, Kansas City, 1988.

Living Faith: An Introduction to Theology (co-authored with Gloria Thomas), Kansas City, 1989.

Hard Decisions: Forgoing and Withdrawing Artificial Nutrition and Hydration, Kansas City, 1990.